MANAGING THE INTERVIEW

A How-To-Do-It Manual for Hiring Staff

SUSAN CAROL CURZON

*HOW-TO-DO-IT MANUALS
FOR LIBRARIANS*

Number 47

NEAL-SCHUMAN PUBLISHERS, INC.
New York, London

Published by Neal-Schuman Publishers, Inc.
100 Varick Street
New York, NY 10013

Printed and bound in the United States of America.

Library of Congress Cataloging-in-Publication Data

Curzon , Susan Carol .
   Managing the interview : a how - to - do - it manual / by Susan C .
Curzon .
     p.   cm . -- (A How-to-do-it manual ; no . 47)
   Includes index .
   ISBN 1-55570 - 160 -4
   1 . Employment interviewing .   I . Title . II . Series : How-to-do-it
manuals for libraries ; no . 47 .
HF5549 . 5 . I6C87 1995
658 . 3 ' 1124 -- dc20   94 - 47336
                                     CIP

To my Aunt and Uncle, Joan and Marty Yudoff,
for their years of support and affection.

CONTENTS

INTRODUCTION

What makes some organizations motivated and dynamic and others tedious and uninspired? Why are some organizations filled with staff capable of meeting every challenge while others have staff resistant to any change? How do some organizations gain reputations as a great place to work while others are regarded as a last chance job?

The answer lies in the quality of the staff. With a good staff, an organization can excel. Good staff provides good service and products, makes the right decisions and is filled with new ideas. They have team spirit, and bring dedication and vitality to every phase of the operation. Good staff is the critical factor in an organization's achievement of its goals.

The question is: how does an organization get good staff? The answer seems simple: hiring the best people for the job. However, hiring the best people is not easy. Effective hiring depends upon our ability to manage an interview and our ability to determine during the interview how well that particular candidate will perform on the job. But how can we tell during the brief period of the interview if the candidate is the right person? How can we be sure that we are really understanding the candidate's skills and abilities during the interview process? How do we manage an interview so that we have a consistently successful outcome?

Fortunately for us all, managing a good interview is not something we have to be born with. An understanding of the interview process can be learned. The techniques necessary to uncover the best candidate in the interview are techniques that can be learned.

This book was written to help you develop the needed skills to manage the interview. Starting at the time when the applications for the position are on your desk, the book's eight chapters explore, point by point, the process of preparing for the interview, creating the questions, conducting the interview, evaluating the candidate and offering the job. Each chapter examines an aspect of the interview process in detail to help the reader develop the skill and the understanding needed to interview and hire the best candidate for the job.

OVERVIEW

CHAPTER 1 PREPARING FOR THE INTERVIEW

Point 1: Screen the candidates.
Point 2: Determine the number of candidates to interview.
Point 3: Decide upon the length of the interview.
Point 4: Set the interview date.
Point 5: Create a positive image.
Point 6: Create the proper physical setting.
Point 7: Decide on taping the interview.
Point 8: Notify the applicants.
Point 9: Confirm the interviews the day before.
Point 10: Don't promise the job ahead of time.
Point 11: Set the interview day up properly.

CHAPTER 2 CREATING THE QUESTIONS

Point 1: Structure the interview.
Point 2: Base the questions on the job.
Point 3: Prepare the answers.
Point 4: Ask probing questions.
Point 5: Phrase the questions appropriately.
Point 6: Ask situational questions.
Point 7: Cover the basic questions.
Point 8: Ask the right number of questions.
Point 9: Avoid illegal questions.
Point 10: Prepare questions based on your screening notes.
Point 11: Keep the questions confidential.

CHAPTER 3 USING A GROUP OR PANEL INTERVIEW PROCESS

Point 1: Select a good panel.
Point 2: Choose the right number of people for the panel.
Point 3: Decide whether to go inside or outside for the panel.
Point 4: Treat the panelists as guests.
Point 5: Orient the panel.
Point 6: Excusing the panel.
Point 7: Gather back all the test materials.

Point   3: Evaluate the educational background.
Point   4: Gamble on inexperience with potential.
Point   5: Evaluate the answers.
Point   6: Consider the work group.
Point   7: Avoid early decisions.
Point   8: Don't compare the candidate with yourself.
Point   9: Don't focus on a single piece of information.
Point 10: Be aware of personal biases.
Point 11: Evaluate body language.
Point 12: Be aware of false notions.
Point 13: Don't falsely compare candidates.
Point 14: Do not discriminate against the pregnant candidate.
Point 15: Know why the candidate wants to change jobs.
Point 16: Watch for chronology.
Point 17: Examine the candidate's career.
Point 18: Determine how interested the candidate is.
Point 19: Remember no one is perfect.
Point 20: Don't let ego get in the way.
Point 21: Consider diversity in the workplace.
Point 22: Simulate the candidate in the workplace.
Point 23: Evaluate the candidate's questions.
Point 24: Review basic behavior.
Point 25: Don't feel sorry for the candidate.
Point 26: Remember skills develop but attitudes never change.
Point 27: Check references.
Point 28: Sleep overnight on the decision.
Point 29: Hire only when satisfied.
Point 30: Make the tough choices.
Point 31: Maintain records.

CHAPTER 7 OFFERING THE JOB

Point   1: Prepare the offer.
Point   2: Negotiate salary effectively.
Point   3: Approach the candidate properly.
Point   4: Compete effectively with other offers.
Point   5: Accepting no for an answer.
Point   6: Negotiate the start date.
Point   7: Give time for consideration.
Point   8: Make special arrangements.
Point   9: Demonstrate courtesy.
Point 10: Confirm in writing.

CHAPTER 8 WRAPPING UP

Point 1: Inform all candidates who were not selected.
Point 2: Inform all candidates in a timely fashion.
Point 3: Announce the appointment.
Point 4: Manage hostile responses.
Point 5: Manage special concerns.
Point 6: Evaluate the interview.

1 PREPARING FOR THE INTERVIEW

POINTS TO REMEMBER

Point 1: Screen the candidates.
Point 2: Determine the number of candidates to interview.
Point 3: Decide upon the length of the interview.
Point 4: Set the interview date.
Point 5: Create a positive image.
Point 6: Create the proper physical setting.
Point 7: Decide on taping the interview.
Point 8: Notify the applicants.
Point 9: Confirm the interviews the day before.
Point 10: Don't promise the job ahead of time.
Point 11: Set the interview up properly.

PREPARING FOR THE INTERVIEW

The picture that comes to mind most often when we think of the interview is two people sitting opposite each other in a private room. One is asking the questions and evaluating the answers, the other is working hard to appear poised and ready with the right answers. The fact is that the actual face to face interview is only one part of a much longer interview process.

Actually, we should think of a theatre production when we think of managing the interview. When an audience sees a play on opening night, they often admire the beauty of the set, the ease of the performers, and the cleverness of the writing. A theatre production, viewed by the audience, appears to happen as if by magic. However, as we all know, a great deal of work has occurred to bring the production to life. Writers, stage managers, set designers, actors, and directors have been busy for months working out every part of the play so that there will be a successful debut. When we think about managing an interview, we should think about managing a play production. An interview is like a play in which the actual face to face interview is the only part that the audience sees. Behind the scenes, staff have been preparing the production details for weeks to make sure that the interview is successful.

When an interview goes well it is not just because we are skilled at asking questions and interpreting the answers but also because the frame, the structure, and the process of the interview has been properly prepared. The physical setting of the interview, the notification of the candidates, the interview dates and times are all as much a part of the interview process as the interview itself. It is important for us to be attentive to the details of the interview process so that the interview can proceed smoothly. When an interview process is well-run, candidates have a better chance of succeeding and we have a better chance of evaluating the candidates in a good light. Additionally, a well-managed interview sends a message to the candidates about the professionalism of the organization.

Remember the reward for working through the preparation phase is the pleasure that you will have in obtaining the best possible candidate for the position!

Let's look now at the first phase of managing the interview—preparation.

POINT 1: SCREEN THE CANDIDATES.

The first step in preparing for the interview is to screen the candidates that have applied for the position in order to determine which of the candidates will be interviewed for the job. Candidates are screened in or out of the interview by reviewing certain elements, which we will look at shortly, on the application form and the resume. As you screen the candidates, have a blank sheet of paper on your desk so that you can begin to take notes on anything that you will want to ask the candidate. That information will be used later when you create the questions for the interview.

BASIC INFORMATION

First, look over the applications and resumes to make sure that all of the basic information is there for you to begin the screening process. Every candidate should have provided name, address, phone, work history, special certificates, if any, and educational level. These basic elements have to be available in order for you to proceed with the screening process. It is a reasonable expectation that a candidate would provide this basic information. At this point, you could disqualify any candidate who did not provide this basic information either on the application or on the resume.

MINIMUM REQUIREMENTS

Next, look at the applications and resumes to see which candidates meet the minimum requirements for the job. Every job has some minimum requirements. Usually there is some educational level, special certificates or work experience without which the candidate could not do the job. Check to see if those minimum requirements have been met by the candidates. Now, you might be in the type of organization, usually in the public sector, that mandates minimum requirements of education, certificates or years of experience for a job. When a minimum requirement is mandated it means, for example, that the lack of a degree or a certain number of years of experience might completely disqualify a candidate. If this is your situation, make sure that all of the minimum requirements are met. If some candidates accidentally get by without meeting mandated minimum requirements and that oversight is discovered later on, you could end up with a contested interview and unnecessary delays.

If there is no set policy on minimum requirements, then it is to your advantage to have flexibility and to be able to use your own judgment as to whether or not a candidate is qualified for the job. One word of caution. Be careful that you do not compromise too much in what may reasonably be minimum expectations of education and experience for the job. Lowering of requirements may send an unintentional signal to your boss or to the personnel office that the job does not have a certain level of value and may not require the salary that you want it to have.

JOB EXPERIENCE

After reviewing the minimum requirements, look over the work experience of each of the candidates to see who can handle the job. Does the career history of the candidate indicate that your job is the next logical step? Do the skills of the candidate match with what you are requiring? Do the candidate's job experiences provide enough relevancy to this job? Has there been progressive responsibility or progressive specialization that will be of interest to you? Is there every indication that the candidate can perform on the job?

Look at other types of interesting experiences too. Is there some unusual body of experience in the resume that would be of interest to you? Experiences such as extensive foreign travel, fellowships, cultural and language fluency or publications might add up to a candidate that will be worth looking at. Consider interviewing candidates with interesting backgrounds even if their work history may not be as extensive as others'. Candidates with an unusual background will often bring a different and exciting dimension to the job.

Be broad, not narrow, in your interpretation of a candidate's experience. Look at experiences that may not be exactly what you expected but which could cross over into the job. For example, a person who has limited job experience but who has held office in a variety of community organizations probably has developed organizational and speaking skills that might be useful to you.

Don't let false assumptions influence the screening process. For example, just because a person has spent all their lives in one type of organization does not mean that they cannot work in another. Look at the skills and experiences of the candidate not just at their work location. Such false assumptions often make us lose good candidates.

CHRONOLOGY

Go back now to pay careful attention to the dates on the application form and resume. Any chronology that does not follow a normal pattern should be a red flag to you.

Look to see what jobs each candidate has had in the last few years. Watch for three things—the amount of jobs, the duration of the jobs and long absences from work. Sometimes there is a legitimate explanation for job hopping but sometimes frequent job changes can also reveal immaturity, a history of employee problems, or some serious physical, mental or home problems.

Look now at the educational record. Has any candidate attended school for an unusually long time? Were there many schools attended? Again, sometimes candidates are putting themselves through school, stopping to have kids or caring for aging parents but sometimes there is a lack of discipline, follow-through or commitment.

Try not to prejudge unusual education and career chronologies since there can be many legitimate causes for people not to follow more regular life patterns. However, if you have a candidate that you want to interview who has an irregular chronology, do make a note so that you can ask about it during the interview.

CAREER PROGRESS

Look closely now at the progression of each candidate's career. First, scan the career path to see if each candidate is going up or down the career ladder. Then, compare each candidate's current job with the one you are trying to fill. Is your job a step up? A step down? A step across for the candidates?

If your job is a step up for any candidate, it is a pretty safe assumption that the candidate is just trying to advance. Usually, we should screen in this candidate, all other qualifications being well, because an ambitious person brings a lot of motivation and energy to the job.

If your job is a step down for any candidate, there might be several causes. First, the candidate might have realized that he or she was not suited for a higher level position. Second, there might be a threat of a layoff in which case the candidate needs to get into another job fast. Third, the candidate might have reviewed his or her life and decided to spend more time with friends and family rather than with the demands of a higher level job. Fourth, the candidate might be in danger of being fired for a problem at work. Lastly, the candidate might be burned out and looking for an easier position. If you decide to interview the candidate, you certainly would want to explore thoroughly why the candidate wants to take a downward career change.

If your job is a step across for any candidate, check for these causes. Has the candidate plateaued in his or her current job? The number of years that the candidate has been in that job is often an indicator of plateauing. Candidates who have plateaued might be hoping that they might have a chance to get ahead in a different organization even if they start out by being in a similar job. If you decide to interview the candidate, you will have to determine whether or not the candidate lacked opportunity for advancement or lacked ability to advance. Candidates who are stepping across might also be looking just for a change of scenery. Sometimes a candidate might not be that ambitious but just feels the need for change. A candidate who is stepping across might also be under threat of a layoff too. Again, if you want to interview this candidate, be sure to explore thoroughly the reasons that the candidate has for a job change.

One clear indication of the path of a candidate's career is the salary history. Look to see whether it is going up or down also. If it is going down, ask the candidate why.

Also check the reasons why each candidate has left his or her previous jobs. Are the reasons sound? Does anything appear to be covered up or avoided? Also correlate the reasons for leaving various positions with the salary level. Does the salary make sense for the reasons that were given? For example, if a candidate gave "advancement in career" as a reason for leaving but the salary level went down on the new job, there is the possibility of a problem.

EDUCATION

Review the educational level of each candidate. What is the highest educational level achieved? Are there any special certificates or distinctive competencies? Any fluency in foreign languages? Does the candidate go to workshops or trade or professional conferences?

In short, see if the person shows a pattern of growth through education. A person who is constantly growing and learning new things will be an asset on the job.

PRESENTATION

Consider also the presentation of the application form and the resume of each candidate. Is it neat and orderly? Does it show structure and organized thinking? Sloppy, messy work, typos or inaccurate and incomplete information may give you an idea of the person's work habits.

WORK SAMPLES

Next, look at the work samples if you requested any. It is not uncommon in jobs that are creative to ask the candidates to bring or send work samples. This will give an idea of the work that the candidates can really do on the job. Samples of art work, photos of displays, news releases, or grants may all indicate the calibre of the work.

When reviewing the work samples, look at aspects such as the creativity, the quality of the presentation, the choice of items, the ability of the sample to speak well of the candidates, or the level of writing in any of the documents.

One real problem with work samples is that they are more often requested than used. If you have requested them, do take the time to review them. As a special courtesy, you should have the work samples in the interview and should refer to them or ask questions about them.

An additional special courtesy is to give all the candidates an opportunity to pick up their work samples after the conclusion of the interview process—some of these samples are difficult or costly to duplicate and the candidates will appreciate getting them back even if they did not get the job.

TAKING NOTES

Finally, this is just to remind you again to make notes on anything puzzling, unusual, outstanding or different about the applicants so that you can ask questions during the interview. If candidates are not asked about experiences that are interesting or puzzling, you will be left with that nagging feeling of uncertainty about the candidates. That nagging feeling will cloud the decision-making later when the time comes to choose the candidate. Sometimes we pass over a good candidate because of that nagging feeling of doubt when the doubt could have been resolved within the interview.

POINT 2: DETERMINE THE NUMBER OF CANDIDATES TO INTERVIEW.

Count up the number of candidates that you have decided to screen in so that you know how many people you will be interviewing. The number of eligible candidates determines the length of the interview schedule.

One word of caution should be mentioned when determining the number of candidates. Be careful not to set an arbitrary amount on the number of candidates who will be interviewed. The only factor that should determine the number of candidates to be interviewed is how many are qualified for the position. For example, it is not wise to say, "we only have one morning to interview so we will only see four candidates." It could be that the fifth or the sixth candidate might be the one for the job.

Sometimes it does happen that you will have an excessive number of qualified candidates for a job. In this case, it is better to apply tougher screening requirements, then to create an arbitrary number to interview.

POINT 3: DECIDE UPON THE LENGTH OF THE INTERVIEW.

The length of time of the actual interview should be determined in advance. It is important to set a target length for the interview for many reasons. First of all, you have to know how far apart to schedule the candidates. Next, you have to know how much time you need to set aside on your own schedule. If your office is not adequate for an interview or you do not have an office, you need to know the length of time so that you can reserve a confidential room in which the interview can be conducted. Lastly, the candidates themselves need to know how much time to set aside. Obviously, it is essential that candidates should know in advance whether they will be at the interview site one hour or one day. In short, there are many logistical issues that depend upon the length of the interview.

How should we arrive at the best length for an interview? Most importantly, the duration of the interview depends upon what the interview must accomplish. In other words, the time frame of the interview should be controlled by whatever needs to be accomplished during the interview. If the interview is too short, there is a risk of not getting adequate information from the candidate. Since every decision is only as good as the information upon which it is based, inadequate information during an interview might lead to a faulty decision about the candidate.

The duration of the interview should be appropriate to the level of the person that is being hired. In general, a rule of thumb is that the greater the impact the person will have on the organization, the longer the interview will be.

It is important not to force the interview into a false time frame. Do not say "I only have the morning to interview so I can only give each candidate fifteen minutes." Instead, let the length of the interview be determined by the amount of information needed from the candidate.

When considering the length of time, be sure to take into account the time needed after each interview in which you can reflect upon the strengths and weaknesses of each candidate. When we rush pellmell through each candidate, with no time in between for thought, there is a risk of overlooking important information or confusing which candidate said what. The interview is no time for snap judgments and quick impressions. Give yourself time to think through the abilities of the candidates.

Make sure in scheduling that the candidates do not feel rushed. Never treat candidates as if they were in a cattle call. They will resent it. Additionally, if there are too many candidates, in too short a time frame, the candidates will soon become a blur to you.

Having said all this, be careful not to schedule the interview for too long a period of time. Interviews that drag on and on do no one a service. You and the candidate will become bored.

However, do retain some degree of flexibility in the length of the interview. Some candidates have more to say. They may have more experience or may be more talkative. Some are very clipped and concise and may need only half the time. You have to move with the flow of the interview.

POINT 4: SET THE INTERVIEW DATE.

Early on, the actual date for the interview should be set. The date of the interview is critical for your schedule, the schedule of the candidates and of the staff who may be assisting in the process.

Be sure to set the date for a reasonable time ahead. If the date is too soon, you may run into scheduling problems with the candidates. While it is true that candidates, motivated for a job, will do almost any kind of re-scheduling, it is important to be reasonable with the date. Higher level candidates might have commitments that are difficult to re-schedule. Candidates coming from out-of-town must make the appropriate arrangements. Professionals might need to prepare for the job by reading annual reports, visiting the site or gathering other information. All of this takes time and it makes for a better interview if the time is allowed.

However, be aware of the danger of setting the interview too far away in time. Candidates who are looking for jobs are usually hunting for a position pretty seriously and may, in a few weeks time, accept a new position. Additionally, an interview that is set many weeks from the job ad and initial contact sends a distinct message that either you are not interested in the candidate or that there is trouble with the position. If you find yourself in the difficult position of setting an interview date far from what is reasonable, it is best to send a letter to the candidates to let them know what is going on. Most candidates would rather know what is happening than disappear into the black hole of applications for a position.

Even when the date of the interview is set, be sure to maintain some flexibility or, at least, have a back-up date. Occasionally, there will be an excellent candidate who truly cannot make the date set. Do not lose out on a good candidate because of a lack of flexibility. Yet, one should be wary of the candidate who requires too much flexibility. A candidate who does not seem to be able to make any date might not have the interest and motivation for the job. No one should be placed in the position of having to beg a candidate to come to the interview. Candidates who have so much ambivalence about the job herald future problems. Let them go and move on to other candidates. The problem is that sometimes it is difficult to tell who is legitimately having problems with the dates and who really does not want to come for the interview. About the only way that you can tell is by assessing the reasons that a candidate offers for not being able to make the date. Legitimate candidates are usually very forthcoming about their scheduling conflicts and will tell you why there is a problem. You have to judge whether or not to accommodate the candidate or remove the candidate from the interview process.

POINT 5: CREATE A POSITIVE IMAGE.

Always have in mind the importance of creating a positive image throughout the interview process. The candidates, whether hired or not, should feel very satisfied with their treatment and with the process. Even the staff helping out with the interview process should learn from the experience and have pride in the way that the organization conducts itself.

Make a continual effort to maintain the highest standards of professionalism. Create a positive image in the minds of everyone involved in the hiring process.

POINT 6: CREATE THE PROPER PHYSICAL SETTING.

Surprisingly, many interviews are conducted in an unacceptable setting. A good interview should put candidates at ease and should transmit to them a sense of pride and professionalism. It is difficult to do this in a room that is bare, noisy, messy, or uncomfortably arranged.

Create for the candidate the proper physical setting. Choose a room that has enough space, is physically attractive, comfortable, and well-lit. The room should not intrude into the interview but instead should be a comfortable backdrop to the process.

First, give some thought to the seating. Often, in an effort to be informal, we place the candidates on too soft sofas or other low chairs that are hard to get in or out of. Such furniture makes candidates uncomfortable. It is difficult for candidates to relay a crisp professional image when they are sunk deep into a sofa.

Consider also the spacing of the furniture. If you will be sitting at a table or around a desk, allow leg room. Additionally, provide enough space between you and the candidate so that individual spatial needs are respected. This is particularly important with strangers who usually need more space than people who are familiar with each other.

Do not forget the positioning of the furniture. Allow the candidate to face you. If candidate and interviewer are side by side or at a difficult angle, the candidate will be unable to transmit comfortable body language or proper eye contact.

Try to see the room from the candidates' eyes. Sit in their seat and simulate how it feels. Is there a glare in their eyes from the windows? Is there a distracting background? Is there enough space for good movement? If not, make changes until the room is comfortable. Be particularly careful with glassed-in rooms where candidates will not only have a lot of other visual stimuli but also will be aware of being seen.

Next, make sure that the room is confidential. No one should be able to overhear the interview. If candidates feel that they can be overheard and, moreover, if they can hear a lot of other sound, it is very upsetting to them. Apart from the fact that it is distracting, it also makes them feel insecure because of the potential for so many others to listen. Often, candidates who are not in a confidential setting also feel demeaned as if their interview was not worthy of the respect of confidentiality. Questions and answers should not be heard by anyone outside of the interview.

Make sure that you consider the needs of persons with disabilities. If you know in advance that you have a person interviewing who has a disability, make sure that the person has space for a wheelchair, crutches, a seeing-eye dog, or anything else that might require additional space. While no persons with disabilities want you to fall all over them solicitously, you can just make quiet arrangements so that they too have the opportunity to move easily about the room.

Lastly, make sure that the room is immaculate. Stacked up chairs, loose files, dirty coffee mugs and waist-deep in-baskets are all an unacceptable backdrop to the interview. Show the candidate complete respect with an interview setting that is completely professional.

POINT 7: DECIDE ON TAPING THE INTERVIEW.

A number of interviews, particularly in the public sector, are being audio-taped. Often, this is an organizational policy and, unless you own the business, you may not have much to say about whether to tape or not. The benefit of taping is that it protects both the interviewers and the candidates. In the event of a protest of the interview, there is a record of what actually was said and done.

The candidates must know up front if the interview will be taped. Initially, people feel a little nervous and awkward about being taped but often that feeling soons wears off as the presence of the tape recorder recedes behind the importance of the interview. I usually avoid taping though if I do not have too because it can intrude upon the interview and bring a certain formality to the process. People do tend to proceed with more caution than necessary when taping is going on.

POINT 8: NOTIFY THE APPLICANTS

All candidates should be notified as to whether or not they were screened in or out. It is important that all candidates receive a letter or phone call informing them of their status.

Let's look first at how to notify the candidates who were screened in. These candidates should receive a phone call which will let them know in a warm and friendly fashion that they were screened in. This phone call should establish if the candidates are still interested in the job. Some basics can also be reviewed at this time, for example, a discussion regarding the date of the interview, the duration of the interview and any supplemental information that may be required from the candidate.

Then the candidates should receive a letter of information. While the tone remains pleasant and welcoming, the letter must convey the time, length, date and place of the interview. This letter should also let the candidates know if there is anything special that they should bring with them to the interview.

Candidates from out of town should have travel and hotel information and whether you are paying for it or not. Additionally, arrangements should be made to pick candidates up at the airport or at the hotel if needed. Anyone driving to the interview should have maps and parking stickers if necessary. The candidates will appreciate the care that is being taken to put them at ease.

The letter that is sent to candidates who were not screened in is equally important. This letter should have an equally warm tone and should thank the candidates for their interest. Of course, the letter should be as non-committal as possible. At no time should any reasons be given in writing as to why the candidates were screened out. If you feel that there are candidates who should be encouraged to apply for other positions at a later date, go ahead and encourage them but be sure that the letter does not sound as if there are any future promises. Do not encourage candidates that you would never be interested in just to make the candidates feel better when they receive the letter. It does neither the candidate nor the organization any service to give a false message to the candidate.

Be sure that the letters screening candidates out are sent in a timely fashion. Candidates who hear that they were not screened in until weeks afterwards tend not to be very happy. This discourtesy is cruel and reflects badly on the reputation of the organization and yourself. Be careful not to send the letters out too fast either. There are no candidates who want to know by return mail that they were not qualified for the interview. Please think of the person's feelings.

Sometimes a telephone call can be made telling candidates that they were not successful. However, since this can be hard on both you and the candidates, a phone call is best reserved for someone that you know well. If you feel the need for something more personal for a particular candidate, write a personal note at the bottom of the formal letter. This helps to soften the blow.

You should be prepared to receive one or two phone calls from candidates who were screened out asking why they were not successful. Generally, it is better not to get into these discussions too deep with candidates. Such conversations, particularly with a stranger, rarely end well. While sometimes the candidate really wants to know the reason so that their future efforts will be successful, more often than not the candidate will begin to debate your decision. Obviously, such a conversation has to be cut off which leaves both parties with an awkward feeling. If you do get such a call, stress the candidate's good points and indicate areas in which there could be more education or experience if appropriate. Keep this conversation at a very general and very pleasant level. The only exception to this procedure is when the candidate sincerely wants some career advice and you know the candidate well and desire to help him or her. If this occurs, invite the candidate in for a conversation and give your most honest and most positive advice. Of course, it is best to have this conversation a couple of weeks at least after the interview. That way, the candidate is more focused on the future not on the recent disappointment of not getting the job.

FIGURE 1-1: Sample Letters—When the candidate is screened in for the job

Oceans Unlimited
75 Water Lane
Malibu, Ca. 91359

Mr. Nathan Essey
42 Riverfront Road
Annapolis, Maryland 21037

Dear Mr. Essey:

We look forward to interviewing you for the position of Oceanographer. The interview will take place on Wednesday, June 17th, at 10 A.M. at 75 Water Lane in Malibu. I enclose a map and a parking permit for the employee lot.

The interview will be about one hour. We would like to review your work experience, your education and your qualifications for the job. Assisting me with the interview will be Ms. Sara Hernandez who is the Assistant Director of the Department of Environmental Concerns.

You should plan on arriving fifteen minutes ahead of the interview as there is some additional paperwork for you to fill out.

Please call me or my assistant, Andrew Paalos, at 314-687-5959 if you have any questions about the interview.

I look forward to seeing you on the 17th.

Very truly yours,

Josselyn Donnelly
Director

FIGURE 1-2:   Sample Letter—For candidates who were not screened in:

Oceans Unlimited
75 Water Lane
Malibu, Ca. 91359

Mr. Andrew Casper
978 Rutherford St.
Philadelphia, Pa. 67845

Dear Mr. Casper:

    This is to thank you for your interest in the position of Oceanographer with our company. While we will be interviewing other candidates for the position, we did appreciate your consideration of us for a position.
    We wish you every good fortune in your job search.

Very truly yours,

Josselyn Donnelly
Director

POINT 9: CONFIRM THE INTERVIEWS THE DAY BEFORE.

We are often surprised at the number of people who do not show up for an important interview without even the courtesy of calling. Sudden blank spots in a carefully planned schedule are very inconvenient for everyone involved with the interview. In order to avoid this situation as much as possible, it is a good practice to call the candidates a day or so before the interview to confirm their attendance. Of course, it is true that people should demonstrate the necessary motivation for the job and should not need a reminder. However, these "no shows" are a fact of life and it will make the interview day easier if the cancellations are known ahead of the interview day. Naturally, it is too late to re-schedule the other candidates but sometimes candidates who show up earlier can be taken in advance of their scheduled time.

POINT 10: DON'T PROMISE THE JOB AHEAD OF TIME.

Never promise the job to any candidate ahead of the interview process. You may have a favorite candidate but may not reveal to anyone, including the favorite candidate, who that person is. You need to keep an open mind about all the candidates. Let's look at why promising the job ahead of time is a bad practice.

First of all, you have a responsibility to maintain the integrity of the organization. If you want your organization to have an open, honest, and honorable environment, then you have to support that environment through all your actions. If we are dishonest with candidates and go through an interview process with a job already promised, it will damage the openness of the culture and send a clear message to staff that it is acceptable to work behind "closed doors". Now, if you think that the promise will remain a secret, there is a surprise waiting for you. Word gets out and the knowledge of that promise tells staff that the interview process is nothing and that it can be subverted. The cumulative results, over the long-term, of an under-handed environment is one in which very few of us would care to live.

Secondly, you must be careful to preserve your own reputation. If you become known as someone who plays games in the work environment, staff will grow wary and may cut you off from meaningful and productive communication. Additionally, if you are in a profession or an area which is relatively small or well-connected, you may find that fewer and fewer top candidates are attracted to any positions that may report to you knowing that the jobs are usually promised ahead of time. This is a heavy price to pay for the want of a little integrity.

Next, promising the job ahead of time usually backfires in our face. Many times people have promised positions only to discover that someone brand new who has interviewed for the job is actually much better. It is a real predicament to find out that the favorite candidate is not the best one on the list. When this occurs, you are faced with two possibilities. The first is to take the favored but lesser candidate knowing that better could have been done for the organization. The other is to break a promise, hire the new candidate and face public exposure and probably a grievance from the favorite and now angry candidate. Neither spectre is very appealing for a person with any sense.

Consider also how unfair it is to call together a variety of candidates, to create cost in the hiring process, to incur expenses for the candidates as they take time off work and drive or fly to the interview when you have promised a candidate ahead of time. If you want to get a feel for how wrong this is, just imagine yourself as a candidate who has gone to all of the trouble to interview only to discover that the candidate was pre-selected.

One problem that occurs from time to time is when your boss promises the job ahead of time. This is an extremely awkward situation for all parties involved. If you are told by your boss that the job is promised or, worse, find out from someone else, you do need to speak with your boss about the extent and explicitness of the commitment. If the boss has made a commitment and intends to stick by it, you can either choose to buck the boss, complain to your boss' supervision or to comply. The first two choices places your job at risk, the latter choice, your integrity. Additionally, if you go with the favorite candidate of your boss, you have an employee on your hands who is comfortable making end runs around you. This dilemma leaves you no avenue of escape. You can continue to work with your boss in the hopes that he or she will have a change of mind particularly if you can find a way that shows that your way is in everyone's best interests. You could also see if there is something else that the boss' favorite candidate can do that would be an advancement for that candidate and still save face for your boss. Otherwise, keep your fingers crossed that the boss' choice would be the top choice anyway.

In promising the job ahead of time, we have everything to lose and little to gain.

POINT 11: SET THE INTERVIEW DAY UP PROPERLY.

A key ingredient in having a successful interaction between you and the candidates is to control all of the logistics of the interview day. An interview process that is smooth and untroubled gives everyone a sense of confidence. When all of the logistical issues have been properly handled, everyone can relax and focus on the interview itself. When logistical issues are not dealt with or are dealt with poorly, they intrude into the interview process and waste time that is needed for the candidates.

First of all, on the day of the interview, do a last check and make sure that the room is set up properly. Take one last look to make sure that is clean, pleasant and well-arranged.

Additionally, make sure that all hospitality items are available. Coffee should be set up for the candidates if that is appropriate in your setting. Make sure that all parking passes needed are either sent out in advance or made available.

Look to see that all of the tools of the interview are ready. You will need a pencil, a notepad, the questions, a tape recorder and spare tape if you are going to tape. If your organization requires formal scoring and has a difficult way of scoring interviews, be sure to have a calculator available too. Don't be scrambling for these things as the candidate is shown in the door.

Lastly, have a last minute conversation with the clerical staff to make sure that they are ready to receive the candidates. They should know how to greet the candidates, where to seat them and what, if anything, they need to give them to fill out. Remind staff not to disturb you with phone calls or messages so that the rapport between the candidates and you is undisturbed. Once again, none of this should be done at the last minute.

CONCLUSION

Sometimes you may feel mired in detail during the process of preparing for the interview. It helps to remember that the successful management of many details makes for a successful outcome. Think again about our image of a play in production. Concentrate on making each element of the interview effective in order to ensure that the moment of the interview is professional and positive.

PREPARING FOR THE INTERVIEW

QUICK CHECK

Point 1: Screen the candidates.

- Has the application form been completely filled out?
- Have the minimum requirements been met?
- Does the person have some out of the ordinary experiences?
- Are any issues with the dates of employment or education?
- Was the salary progression and promotional history analyzed?
- Is the presentation of the resume neat and orderly?
- Did you take notes on anything that you needed to ask about?

Point 2: Determine the number of candidates.

- Did you avoid setting arbitrary numbers of candidates to interview?

Point 3: Decide upon the length of the interview.

- Have you determined what needs to be accomplished in the interview?
- Has the interview been forced to fit an arbitrary schedule?
- Is there enough time to evaluate the candidate?

Point 4: Set the interview date.

- Is there enough time for the applications to be returned and for schedules to be set up?
- Is there some flexibility in the schedule?

Point 5: Create a positive image.

- Has the interview created a positive image in the minds of the candidates, panelists and staff?

Point 6: Create the proper physical setting.

- Is the room well-lit, attractive and neat?
- Is the spacing adequate for leg room and personal space?

- Is the furniture well-spaced?
- Is the room confidential?
- Can persons with disabilities move around the room easily?

Point 7: Decide on taping the interview.

- Does the organization have a policy on taping?
- Do you feel comfortable taping?

Point 8: Notify the applicants.

- Did a letter or phone call go to all candidates to inform them of their status?
- Was all of the logistical information given to the candidates who were screened in?
- Were the candidates who were screened out informed in a timely and courteous fashion?

Point 9: Confirm the interviews the day before.

- Were all the candidates called to confirm the interview?

Point 10: Don't promise the job ahead of time.

- Do you want to preserve the integrity of the hiring process?
- Do you want to maintain a reputation for being fair?

Point 11: Set the interview up properly.

- Did you do a last check on the interview room?
- Are all the hospitality items prepared?
- Are the tools of the interview ready?
- Does the staff know what to do when the candidate arrives?

2 CREATING THE QUESTIONS

POINTS TO REMEMBER

Point 1: Structure the interview.
Point 2: Base the questions on the job.
Point 3: Prepare the answers.
Point 4: Ask probing questions.
Point 5: Phrase the questions appropriately.
Point 6: Ask situational questions.
Point 7: Cover the basic questions.
Point 8: Ask the right number of questions.
Point 9: Avoid illegal questions.
Point 10: Prepare questions based on your screening notes.
Point 11: Keep the questions confidential.

CREATING THE QUESTIONS

Of all the elements that have to be managed in the interview process, one of the most critical is the creation of the questions that will be asked during the interview. The questions, and their responses, are the essence of the interview. What we ask during the interview determines what is learned about the candidate. What we learn about the candidate is the basis of our decision about whether or not the candidate will get the job.

Sometimes we are guilty of preparing the questions in too haphazard a manner. Minutes before the interview begins, we pull together a few questions to be asked. When we fall into this habit, there will be a decline in the quality of candidates that are selected. The reason for this decline is simple. If the questions that were asked were not appropriate, not searching enough or not relevant enough for the job, the necessary information about the candidate cannot be obtained. Without the right information, no sound decision about the candidate can be made.

For an effective interview process, we must take the time to create the questions that will elicit the best information about the candidate.

POINT 1: STRUCTURE THE INTERVIEW.

There are many types of interviewing techniques but for the type of interviewing that we are discussing in this book, the structured interview should be used. The structured interview simply means that you have a list of prepared questions that you will ask of each candidate.

Notice that there are two parts to the structured interview. The first is having a list of prepared questions. The second is asking the same questions of each candidate.

Having prepared questions means that we have given some thought to the interview. Instead of walking into the interview and firing questions from the hip, we have already thought about the job and about the type of person that would be best for the job. The more thinking that we have done about the interview and the job, the better the interview process will be.

The second part of the structured interview—asking the same questions of each candidate—means that we will have some basis of comparison of the candidates. We will discuss this in more detail in Chapter 4.

Now, a structured interview should not be confused with a rigid interview. Grimly stating the questions in a fixed order to the candidate with no discussion or interpretation will do no one a service. A good interview should have the tone of a conversation even though it is not a conversation.

Be sure to embellish the structured interview with unstructured components. A loose discussion at the beginning to relax the candidate, a digression from a question when something interesting strikes you, a little humour and some free flow at the end for more information is all acceptable and will provide you with more insight into the candidate's personality as well as making the interview more enjoyable.

POINT 2: BASE THE QUESTIONS ON THE JOB.

It is important for us to understand that we are not just hiring the best candidate but instead are hiring the candidate who is the best for that particular job. The candidate's abilities and personality must be matched to the duties and personality of the job. Once this is understood then it stands to reason that the interview questions, which should elicit an understanding of the candidate's abilities and personality, must be based upon the needs and requirements of the job. In the interview, we must be able to find out if the candidate will be a good match for the position available. Therefore, we must create questions that are based upon the job itself.

To create questions that are based on the job, start by listing the most important skills that anyone coming into this job must have. For example, if the job requires the supervision of fifteen people, then supervisory ability is an important skill. If the job requires work under a tight deadline, then delivering work on time is an important skill. Once this list is made, proceed to base the questions on the most important skills that have been identified. For example, an interview for the job that required supervision of fifteen people would have a question or two on supervision.

Next, capture what may be called the "personality" of the job. The personality of the job needs to match the candidate's personality or there will be an unhappy fit. A lively, social job calls for someone lively and social. A quiet job at a computer all day calls for someone with some degree of patience and quietness. A fast track job needs people who are fast track personalities. Make sure that you are asking questions that will elicit the personality of the candidate so that you can match it against the personality of the job. If you are having any trouble thinking about what skills are critical or what the personality of the job might really be, think about anyone who was successful in the position. A listing of that person's skills and personality might help you to identify important aspects of the job.

Remember—basing the questions on the job itself is critical to the success of the interview!

POINT 3: PREPARE THE ANSWERS.

In the process of preparing the questions, it is also important to prepare the answers. After all, if you do not know what answers are wanted, how will you be able to judge the candidate's responses? Now, this does not mean that you have to write out the answers exactly. Instead, just create a list that will give you the dimensions of an appropriate response. For example, if there is a question about how to handle a problem customer, list on the answer sheet that the candidate should consider aspects such as the appearance of the situation to other customers nearby, the ability to resolve problems and the attitude towards customer service. In other words, just have a general framework available of what would comprise a complete answer.

Having said all this, it is not necessary for us to be rigid about the answers. Candidates, particularly more creative ones, will come up with quite a variety of answers so be flexible if a candidate is not taking quite the approach that is expected. In other words, do not just listen for the answers that you have pre-determined.

Be as flexible as possible when interviewing entry level staff. They may not have the knowledge or experience for the full range of answers that are desired. Instead, judge them on the logic of their response within the framework of their inexperience.

POINT 4: ASK PROBING QUESTIONS

Ask questions that really probe the experiences, attitudes and the work approaches of the candidate. We cannot get to know the candidate well in a brief period of time unless we ask probing questions.

Avoid questions that can be answered with a yes or no or questions that are so run of the mill that any candidate can anticipate or outsmart them. For example, questions such as "do you think you will like the job here?" or "do you think you will like the people in our company?" will not exactly reveal the candidate's skills.

In addition, avoid leading questions from which the candidate can easily anticipate the response that is wanted. For example, the question, "is it important to you to do a good job?" calls for only one answer. It would be a foolhardy candidate that responded "no, I don't take any pride in my work".

Also stay away from questions that reveal your position and your attitudes. For example, if you were to ask "I think that customer service is the most important thing, what do you think?", the candidate would have little choice except to say "yes, I think so too". Remember that the point of the interview is to find out what the candidates' attitudes are. You already know what you think. All candidates, once they sense what you want, will shape their responses appropriately to what you need.

In addition, don't repeat questions that may have been present on the application form. This does not mean that the interview should not start off by an inquiry about the candidate's background. Beginning an interview with a question about background is expected. Just be careful not to repeat in detail information that is already available. You may take up a lot of time in the interview without garnering any new knowledge.

POINT 5: PHRASE THE QUESTIONS APPROPRIATELY.

Questions that dazzle the candidate with their length or stun them with the breadth of your vocabulary are of little use. You are there to seek information. Therefore, the best approach is to be brief, to be clear and to be to the point.

Anything that blocks good communication between the interviewer and the candidate should be avoided because it will lead to a poor interview. The candidate is probably anxious enough without trying to follow complicated questions. Use plain-speaking language.

How do you know if the questions are phrased appropriately? One way is to have a trusted staff member, who will not violate the confidentiality of the questions, try them out. If your staff member has trouble with the questions, probably the candidate will have trouble too. If the questions are too convoluted or too intimidating, the best will not be brought out in the candidate. Moreover, the organization might look a little ridiculous as if something is being proved in the interview.

When phrasing the questions, think about building a relationship with the candidate as opposed to impressing the candidate.

POINT 6: ASK SITUATIONAL QUESTIONS.

Situational questions are one of the best ways to find out how a candidate will function on the job. A situational question is a question that explores the response of the candidate in a given situation. Situational questions can be asked in one of two ways. The first is to create a hypothetical situation and then let the candidates tell how they would solve it. For example, ask "what do you do when a fire is spotted in the building?" or "what do you do when a VIP has complained about customer service?" The candidates' responses should give you an idea of how they will function in a real life situation.

The second type of situational question is one in which the candidate provides the actual situation within the framework of your question. In other words, you would give the candidate a general situation and the candidate would provide the specific real life experience. For example, ask "can you tell us about a time in which you handled an emergency. What happened and what did you do?" or "tell us about the worst customer service problem you ever handled." In other words, you are asking the candidates to draw upon their specific experience to tell how they performed in a given situation. The response of the candidate will give you specifics about the candidate's performance in the past. This technique has one drawback however. The candidate will, at first, have difficulty coming up with a situation or will try to give a very general response. Push for specific examples and specific responses. When the candidate responds with a specific example, you will be rewarded with some detail of how the candidate actually performed on the job.

However, regardless of approach, be sure to ask the candidates what they would do differently today knowing what they know now. After all, it is important to see not just how a candidate performed during the event but also how a candidate has grown from the experience.

POINT 7: COVER THE BASIC QUESTIONS.

There are certain basic areas that are useful to cover in every interview. These areas give us consistently important information. Make sure that you write questions for every interview that covers the following areas:

The relationship between the candidate and the candidate's current co-workers: Find out how well the candidate gets along with current co-workers. Strong relationships may indicate a team player. Poor relationships sometimes indicate a potential for employee conflicts. Of course, sometimes a candidate will just be in a bad setting. In that case, ascertain how maturely the candidate deals with the situation.

The relationship between the candidate and the candidate's current boss: A person who has a good relationship with one boss can usually carry that over to another. A person with a poor relationship might carry that over to you also. Of course, a poor relationship with the boss may or may not be the candidate's fault.

The candidate's career objective: It is important to know where a candidate is going in order to assess if the candidate's goals fit in with what is going on in your own organization. For example, if the candidate wants to be a vice-president for sales, but you have a job in manufacturing with little promotional opportunity, then the candidate and the job will not be a good fit.

The nature of the candidate's work: Details about the candidate's current work will give you a good indication of the candidate's preparation and ability to handle the the job.

Education and experience: Even though you have this information readily available in the application, create a question that asks the candidate about both education and experience. Sometimes the candidate's retelling will bring up new information or will present the information in a different light. You will have the added advantage of seeing what the candidate highlights—a clear indication of the candidate's interest.

The reason for changing jobs: This question is critical. Knowing why a candidate wants to leave and why a candidate wants to work for you is essential. You will need to ascertain if the candidate is fleeing from any problems and you will also need to see if the reasons that the candidate wants to come here makes sense within the framework of the job.

The most unpleasant feature of the candidate's current job: Prepare a question that asks the candidate about the most unpleasant feature of the job that the candidate now has. If the candidate comes up with something which you know is present in this job, then the candidate will soon be unhappy.

The reason the candidate wants to work here: It is important to know what the candidate's motivation is for applying for the job. You will need to check their answers against the reality of the position. The motivation of the candidate needs to be in alignment with the job's or your company's opportunities.

The candidate's knowledge about your organization: The candidate's knowledge about the organization gives you an indication of how well the candidate prepared for the job. Candidates who are well-prepared usually are more motivated, more organized and more competitive. One always has to ask how interested a candidate is in a job when the candidate makes no effort to find out about the company.

Work habits: People vary quite a bit in work habits. You will want to have a sense of a candidate's work habits to know if those habits are compatible with the job. For example, if your vacant job calls for a lot of detailed work but the candidate appears disorganized and unstructured then probably this is not the candidate for you.

POINT 8: ASK THE RIGHT NUMBER OF QUESTIONS.

Of course, there is no perfect number of questions to ask as it depends upon the information that you need from the interview. However, if too few questions are asked, there will not be enough opportunity for you to get to know the candidate. On the other hand, if too many questions are asked, the interview will become too crowded and exhausting. It is better to ask fewer but deeper questions in which the candidate's responses can be probed than to ask a huge array of questions that may elicit only a superficial response. Moreover, if there are too many questions, you might feel under pressure to finish them in the allotted time and might unintentionally hurry the candidate along. This pressure will be detected by the candidate who will hurry the answers in order to meet a perceived time demand.

As a rule of thumb, you can manage to ask between eight to twelve questions in a one hour interview.

POINT 9: AVOID ILLEGAL QUESTIONS.

There are certain questions that, if asked, will violate the law. These laws were created to protect candidates from discrimination. Illegal questions are unfair to the candidate and put the organization and yourself in danger of lawsuits. You must make sure that illegal questions are not asked.

Let's review what can and what cannot be asked during the interview. Here's a quick guide to legal and illegal questions.

1. Name: It is acceptable to ask if the person has worked for your company under a different name. Ask also if there are other names that they go by, for example, nicknames. If you are checking on the candidate's work record, knowing nicknames can be important. Never ask about names in such a way that you would appear to be inquiring into their ancestry or national origin.

2. Marital and Family Status: Don't inquire about marital status, pregnancy, number or age of children, or information about child care arrangements. You can ask if the candidate can meet certain work schedules. Of course, these questions do have to be asked of males and females.

3. Address: Obviously, you can ask for a person's address and how long they have lived there. You cannot ask who else lives with the candidate nor about whether they rent or own. Be careful inquiring about foreign addresses which would indicate national origin.

4. Birthplace, national origin and citizenship: It is not acceptable to ask about birthplace. You can inquire if a person can submit proof of U.S. citizenship if employed. Obviously, you can ask if the person has the legal right to remain and to work in the United States if the candidate is not a citizen. No questions that would indicate the national origin of the candidate nor the candidate's relatives nor ancestors can be asked. You can ask about a person's language fluency but not about whether or not the language was a mother tongue.

5. Age: Never ask ask how old a person is. Minors can be asked if they have proof of age in the form of a work permit.

6. Disabilities: All the applicants can be asked if they are able to carry out all the essential job assignments in a safe manner. You cannot ask general questions about the nature and severity of the handicap.

7. Religion: Advise all candidates as to the working schedule of the job in case it conflicts with religious practices. You cannot ask any questions related to religion.

8. Military record: Asking about the candidate's experience and education while in the service is acceptable. Asking about the type of discharge is not.

9. Education: You can ask virtually any question about a person's education but you cannot ask about the religious, racial or national affiliation of their schooling.

10. Experience: Asking just about any question in this area is acceptable including what countries they may have visited through their jobs.

11. Arrests and Convictions: Don't inquire about arrests. However, the law allows you to inquire into actual convictions that relate reasonably to the job. For example, you can inquire about the three drunk driving convictions if you are hiring a delivery driver. Or you could inquire about the embezzling conviction if you are hiring a bookkeeper. When looking at convictions, take into account how old the person was at the time of the conviction, how many convictions there were and the severity of the convictions.

12. Organizations: It is acceptable to inquire about professional organizations but not about organizations that reveal race, national origin or religious affiliation.

13. Sex: Don't ask questions that would lead to stereotypes or to a prejudgment of physical capabilities. Don't ask about height or strength or anything that would indicate a bias. Of course, the physical nature of the job should be explained with any lifting or pulling that may be required.

14. Photos: Do not ask for a photo during the interview. You may inform the candidate that a photo will be needed after hiring.

5. Relatives: It is acceptable to ask if the candidate has any relatives who already work for the company.

As you can see, most of questions to ask or not to ask are common sense once it is understood that the intent of the law is to avoid discrimination based upon religion, race, color, disability or sex.

The rule of thumb is that the question cannot be asked if the question is not job relevant or if the purpose of the question is to discriminate.

POINT 10: PREPARE QUESTIONS BASED ON YOUR SCREENING NOTES.

Be sure to go back through the notes that you took while you were screening the applications and resumes and see if there was anything that you have not yet captured in your questions. Remember to ask about everything that seemed unusual, distinctive, puzzling or troubling.

POINT 11: KEEP THE QUESTIONS CONFIDENTIAL.

To ensure that the integrity and legality of the interview is not jeopardized, be sure to keep all the questions completely confidential. If the questions are seen by any of the candidates in advance or by anyone who could give the information to the candidates, then the questions should be thrown out. It is not fair to give someone such an advantage and it will skew the results of the interview if one candidate had time to prepare. If you are in the public sector or an organization with more rigid personnel practices, and it was discovered that one of the candidates had prior knowledge of the questions, it is possible that the entire interview process may be thrown out. Therefore, be careful to keep the questions confidential. The only people that should see the questions are the interviewers and a confidential secretary who may be typing up the questions.

FIGURE 2-1: Sample Questions

EXPERIENCE AND SKILLS

1. Please comment on your preparation for this position.
2. Tell us about your work experience.
3. Tell us in more detail about the responsibilities of your current job.
4. Have you ever been faced with a budget crisis? Tell us about it and how you handled it.
5. Please highlight your experience and responsibilities in the area of finance (or personnel, or sales or marketing etc.).
6. Have you ever worked in a multi-cultural environment?
7. Tell us about the most difficult customer you ever handled.
8. What are the areas in which you need additional skills?
9. Tell us what skills you have with the computer.
10. Tell us about your boss' title and job.
11. Please describe a typical day on the job.

ATTITUDE AND PERSONALITY

1. Why are you interested in this position?
2. What are your reasons for leaving your current job?
3. What do you offer this position?
4. What would you gain personally by this job?
5. Can you describe our organization. How would you fit in?
6. What are the things you do best at work?
7. What are the qualities you like best in a boss?
8. What are your long-term goals?
9. Tell us about a time in which you were supportive of your boss even though you both disagreed.
10. Can you give us an example of an emergency that you dealt with?
11. Tell us about something that you did at work that you are especially proud of.
12. What project gave you the most challenge and why?
13. Your daily workload is getting busier and busier, how do you handle it?
14. Give us an example of time in which you were successful communicating with a person who did not like you.
15. Give an example of a goal that you achieved that was very important to you.
16. What would make a person successful on this job?
17. What are you doing in your current job to make yourself more effective?

FIGURE 2-1. Continued

EDUCATION

1. Tell us about your education?
2. Do you have any special certificates?
3. Are you fluent in any languages other than English?
4. What were your best and worst subjects in school?

SUPERVISION

1. Please share with us your management style—can you give us an example of your style.
2. What was one of the biggest mistakes you made in supervision and what did you learn from it?
3. Can you describe a situation in which you handled a serious conflict between employees.
4. How would you motivate an employee who was burned out on the job?

Be sure to ask the candidate at the end. . . .
    Is there anything else you would like to add that would help us to evaluate you as a candidate?

CONCLUSION

Creating the questions is one of the most critical steps in managing the interview. Designing the best questions possible will elicit the most complete answers from the candidate. Since candidates must be judged on their responses, give them questions that will demonstrate fully their skills, abilities, interests and motivation for the job.

CREATING THE QUESTIONS

QUICK CHECK

Point 1: Structure the interview.

- Is there a list of prepared questions?
- Is the interview too rigid?
- Are there some unstructured components in the interview?

Point 2: Base the questions on the job.

- Have the most important skills of the job been identified?
- Were the questions based on the most important skills?
- Are there questions based upon the personality of the job?

Point 3: Prepare the answers.

- Do you know what answers to expect?
- Are you prepared to listen to different answers?
- Are you aware of the special needs of entry level staff?

Point 4: Ask probing questions.

- Have questions that lead to yes or no answers been avoided?
- Have leading questions been avoided?
- Have routine questions been avoided?
- Have questions which indicate your interests been avoided?

Point 5: Phrase the questions appropriately.

- Are the questions straight-forward and to the point?
- Did you try out the questions?
- Did you try to see the questions from the candidate's viewpoint?

Point 6: Ask situational questions.

- Are there hypothetical situations for the candidate?
- Will candidates be asked for their own situations?

Point 7: Cover the basic questions.

- Have you included the basic questions in the interview?

Point 8: Ask the right number of questions.

- Are there enough questions for a good response?
- Is the interview too crowded with questions?
- Will the candidate feel hurried?

Point 9: Avoid illegal questions.

- Have illegal questions been avoided?
- Do all the questions have job relevancy?
- Will any questions be discriminatory?

Point 10: Prepare questions based on your screening notes.

- Did you include questions from the issues from your notes?

Point 11: Keep the questions confidential.

- Has anyone seen the questions that should not have?
- Has every effort been made to keep the questions confidential?

3 USING A GROUP OR PANEL INTERVIEW PROCESS

POINTS TO REMEMBER

Point 1: Select a good panel.
Point 2: Choose the right number of people for the panel.
Point 3: Decide whether to go inside or outside for the panel.
Point 4: Treat the panelists as guests.
Point 5: Orient the panel.
Point 6: Excusing the panel.
Point 7: Gather back all the test materials.

USING A GROUP OR PANEL INTERVIEW PROCESS

Many organizations, particularly those in the public sector, use more than one interviewer to help with the interview process. Using several people, or a panel, as we will call it here, has many advantages. First, there is the advantage of having several points of view about a candidate. One person may see or hear certain things that the other did not. Second, panelists bring different experiences. This means that the candidate will be judged by a wider range of experience than the more narrow range of one interviewer. Third, several people provide more protection for the organization since there is less chance of bias and more witnesses in the event of any problems. Lastly, when two or three people agree on a candidate as opposed to only one, there is a greater likelihood that the candidate is good.

Let's look now at how to use a panel in the interview process.

POINT 1: SELECT A GOOD PANEL.

It is critical that the panel be selected appropriately in order to ensure the best interview process. If there are problems with the panel, there will be problems with the interview. Make every effort to get a panel that will be a real help to you in the interview.

Begin by choosing people who have some understanding or knowledge of the job. It will do you little good to have people on the panel who have no real idea of what the candidate is talking about. This will be particularly important in the technical areas where it is easy to pull the wool over most people's eyes.

Also take into consideration the level of experience of the panelists. The panelists need to have a comparable level of experience as the candidates have and as the vacant position requires. Otherwise, the panelists really will not understand the demands and complexities of the position.

Remember to think about the personalities of the panelists. If your panelists know each other, do they get along with each other? You don't want to have people carrying over earlier conflicts into your interview process.

Always consider how confidential the panelists are. After all, you do not want the panelists discussing some of the very confidential things that they will hear in the interview. Keep people off the panel if they are known gossips.

Don't forget to take affirmative action into consideration when pulling together a panel. Try to have people from other cultures and from the sex opposite from yourself in order to get a richer interview process in which other points of view and talents might be highlighted.

POINT 2: CHOOSE THE RIGHT NUMBER OF PEOPLE FOR THE PANEL.

Two or three people, including yourself, is usually adequate for a panel. Four or more is rather stressful and threatening for all but candidates interested in the higher level jobs. The only reason for having four or more panelists is when the candidate is interested in a job that affects a large area and there are a lot of people who have a lot at stake in getting the right person. Remember though that the more people there are in the room, the less focus there will be on the candidate. Too many people are distracting and may take up too much conversation time.

POINT 3: DECIDE WHETHER TO GO INSIDE OR OUTSIDE FOR THE PANEL.

This point is mainly for those of you in the public sector. Often, the public sector requests people in the same profession but in neighboring jurisdictions to help with an interview process. For example, a city engineer, a city librarian, or a police captain may help another city to interview engineers, librarians, or police officers. This practice is common throughout the public sector but not at all in the private sector where competition and confidentialty are important.

This means that in the public sector, you can decide whether or not you want your panelists to be from outside or inside the organization. Let's look at the pros and cons of each.

There are three main advantages in going with panelists from the outside. First, if you have a lot of candidates from inside the organization, outside panelists will be less biased in rating the candidates. After all, outside panelists will not be as caught up in who are the favorites or in the history of each individual.

Next, outside panelists bring a different range of experiences to the interview. Often, particularly in the public sector where there is considerable employee longevity, organizations can get quite inbred. When organizations are in-bred, there is a tendency to have less different points of view because everyone has been sharing the same experiences for so long. People from the outside will bring other points of view which will enrich the interview process. Outside panelists will see different aspects and talents of the candidates which people inside might not see. This means that you might hire people with different talents which is very healthy for an organization.

Outside panelists are also often necessary if the position is at a high level. You may not have enough people inside your organization who have enough experience to be able to judge the candidates for that job. Outside panelists can help you with this problem.

There are two drawbacks with outside panelists. First, they do not know the organization. This means that you do need to invest time in some orientation for them. However, even with that, they simply cannot learn in a half hour all the ins and outs of your place. Outside panelists cannot judge whether or not a candidate would fit in with the work group, get along with certain clients, interact with particular managers and so forth. While outside panelists can tell you whether or not they think the candidate can do the job, they cannot tell you whether or not the candidate can do the job with some of the specific demands that your organization may have.

The other drawback is one of motivation. Outside panelists are often very good and very concerned with trying to find the best candidate. However, they do not have to live with the consequences of their decision. They know that they are only there for a day whereas you might live with the candidate for years. Therefore, there is a difference in their motivation. They will do a good job but there is nothing at stake for them if the wrong candidate is hired.

Let's look now at using a panel of people from inside the organization. Using an inside panel is easier for you because the inside panel is pretty much ready to go. Your own people do not need an orientation to the organization. They are well-acquainted with the vacant job, the organization's needs and the colleagues with whom the new person will work. Moreover, they already know how the interview process at your site works. In short, they need very little to be ready to help you with the interview.

Inside panelists are usually very motivated. There is something about knowing that the newly hired person might be working beside you for years to come that acts as a real motivator. Therefore, most inside panelists will be very conscientious about trying to get the right person.

Inside panelists also have a commitment to the organization. They know that good people are vital for the survival of the workplace. Since they have an investment in organizational survival, they will do their best to secure the best person.

Another good reason to have inside panelists is employee development. Interviewing from either side of the desk is a learned skill and the more that staff have a chance to help with interviewing, the more their skills will increase. Increased skills in interviewing means that there is more probability that staff will be able to identify good candidates. These good candidates eventually become good employees which are, of course, the lifeblood of any organization.

The disadvantage of inside panelists is bias when there are many inside candidates. Inside people are often very caught up in politics and friendships. When inside panelists are interviewing inside candidates, there is a greater possibility that not everyone will get a fair shake. However, there will be less likelihood of hiring charmers, since people from the inside know the abilities and frailties of inside candidates whereas an outside panel might be more prone to be charmed.

POINT 4: TREAT THE PANELISTS AS GUESTS.

Be sure to treat the panelists as guests. It is important to remember that the panelists, especially those from the outside, are doing you a favor — even if it is a very willing favor. While it is true that people are flattered to be asked to be on a panel, it is also true that they are giving up time out of a busy schedule. Make the day as easy and enjoyable as possible for them.

One way to make the day easy is to provide the panel in advance with information about the interviews. Send a confirming memo about the date, the time and the location of the interview. Attach a description of the position. For outside panelists, include a description of your organization. Let the panelists know how many candidates will be interviewing that day and who they are. Let them know who else will be on the panel. Also inform them if you will be taping the interview.

If the panelists come from the outside, be sure to send·them a map of the location and a parking sticker if needed. Give them approximate driving times. Tell them how to enter the building. Outside panelists will really appreciate these finishing touches which make their day easier.

Do not forget the hospitality issues. If it is a long day, coffee and donuts in the moring, a well-planned lunch and coffee in the afternoon will all be appreciated by the hard-working panel.

POINT 5: ORIENT THE PANEL.

Be sure to invite the panel to arrive about a half hour before the first interview so that they can learn about the vacant job. This is particularly important if you have outside panelists. During the orientation, which does not have to be a formal process, review with the panel the job and the job requirements. Let the panel know what the job is like and what the daily tasks and assignments are. It is critical that the interviewers understand the job because, if they do not, they will not be able to gauge the suitability of the candidate for the job.

If you are in a more formal organization that has scoring or rating sheets for each interview, be sure that the panel knows how to use the sheets. This is particularly important in the public sector in which candidates often have access to the scores and the comments that the panelists wrote. Any irregularity in the scoring sheets could invalidate the interview—a total waste of time for everyone.

Finally, ask the panelists to adhere to high standards when interviewing. Ask them to look for candidates that they themselves would hire tomorrow.

POINT 6: EXCUSING THE PANEL.

Skip this point if you are in the private sector. It is not uncommon in the public sector for the panelists to be asked by personnel officers if they have any bias about any of the candidates that day. If so, sometimes the panelists, who might feel that they cannot do a fair assessment of that candidate, will excuse themselves for that particular interview. It is better for a panelist to be excused than for the interview to be compromised and probably challenged later on by the candidate.

Equally, the candidates are sometimes asked if they feel that any of the panelists will have a bias against them. Once in awhile a candidate will ask for a particular panelist to be excused. This always is a bit awkward and does not reflect well upon the candidate. Still, it is better for a panelist to step aside than to have a challenged interview. Don't let the removal of a panelist influence you against the candidate.

POINT 7: GATHER BACK ALL THE TEST MATERIALS.

The interview is a confidential process so it is important for you to gather back all the interview materials from the panel. Make sure that all the applications, notes taken during the interview and the list of questions are all in your possession at the end of the day. You don't want confidential materials showing up where they shouldn't.

CONCLUSION

Using a panel has many advantages but a panel must be used wisely and appropriately with an understanding of the advantages and disadvantages. Use a panel, particularly, when you want different viewpoints. That is their special strength.

USING A GROUP OR PANEL INTERVIEW PROCESS

QUICK CHECK

Point 1: Select a good panel.

- Do the panelists have knowledge of the job?
- Do the panelists have a similar level of experience as the job?
- Will the panelists get along well?

Point 2: Choose the right number of people for the panel.

- Have you kept the number of panelists to 2 or 3 including yourself?
- Is there a good reason to have four people on the panel?

Point 3: Decide whether to go inside or outside for the panel.

- Do you want different points of view from outsiders?
- Are you concerned with bias from inside panelists?
- Do you have enough people inside who have the right level of experience to help with the interviews?
- Is staff development in interviewing important to you?

Point 4: Treat the panelists as guests.

- Have you sent the panelists an information packet?
- Have you tended to all hospitality issues?

Point 5: Orient the panel.

- Have you provided everyone with an orientation before the interview?
- Did you ask everyone to adhere to high standards?

Point 6: Excusing the panel.

- Is there anyone on the panel who is biased against the candidates?
- Has any candidate asked a panelist not to conduct the interview?
- Have you allowed either of these actions to influence you?

Point 7: Gather back all test materials.

- Did you get all materials about the interview back from the panel?

4 CONDUCTING THE INTERVIEW

POINTS TO REMEMBER

Point 1: Review the application, resume, and questions.
Point 2: Relax and concentrate.
Point 3: Open the interview properly
Point 4: Ask the already prepared questions.
Point 5: Take notes.
Point 6: Be careful interviewing acquaintances and colleagues.
Point 7: Don't tell about the job first.
Point 8: Be prompt.
Point 9: Watch both voice tone and body language.
Point 10: Control the interview.
Point 11: Protect candidates from your biases.
Point 12: Avoid the halo effect.
Point 13: Don't oversell the position.
Point 14: Give the candidate time to respond.
Point 15: Be careful with responses.
Point 16: Let the applicant talk.
Point 17: Don't be nervous.
Point 18: Be flexible with the questions.
Point 19: Repeat questions if necessary.
Point 20: Be fair to people with disabilities.
Point 21: Discern the truth of the responses.
Point 22: Give the candidate time to ask questions.
Point 23: Don't let candidates know how they did.
Point 24: Close the interview properly.
Point 25: Gather up all files.

CONDUCTING THE INTERVIEW

Finally, all of the effort and work of the past few weeks has come down to the moment in time in which the face-to-face interview is about to be conducted. As a result of careful planning, the best candidates are waiting outside your door. Inside your office, everything that is needed for the interview is ready. Of course, all of your careful preparation doesn't mean that you can relax now. The face-to-face interview is a complex process that requires a great deal of skill and needs all of your concentration and effort.

Think about it this way: the actual interview is the core of the hiring process. No matter how long the interview lasts, there is still only a very short period of time in which to assess the worth and value of another person and to make a decision as to whether or not you want to work side by side with that person for many years to come. The right decision can make a lot of difference in the success of an organization. The wrong decision can have serious repercussions. The time during the interview is time to be taken very seriously.

Let's look now at the points that are essential for conducting a good interview.

POINT 1: REVIEW THE APPLICATION, RESUME AND QUESTIONS.

One more time, before each candidate arrives, review the application and resume. It is important to have the candidate's background firmly in mind before the interview begins. Don't waste time during the actual interview scanning the candidate's resume because you've forgotten what you read a week ago. Instead, have the candidate's background in mind and spend the interview time probing for details of the candidate's experience and skill level.

Besides scanning the application and the resume, review the questions that you have created. You want the questions to roll off your tongue as if you were in a conversation. Therefore, look at them again so that the questions are partially memorized.

Lastly, place the resume, the application and the questions at a convenient location near you so that you can refer to them easily and without undue movement during the interview. It is very distracting for the candidate to see you rummaging through papers. It also gives you the appearance of a disorganized person which may put off a good candidate.

POINT 2: RELAX AND CONCENTRATE

Remember to relax and concentrate before you interview any candidate. You already know how important it is to gain as much knowledge as possible about the candidate during the interview process. If you relax and concentrate, you will increase your listening abilities. If you are listening well during the interview, you will pick up the critical verbal and non-verbal communications of the candidate. This information is essential when you are deciding which candidate to hire.

Good interviewing requires presence of mind. All of your mental faculties should be engaged in listening, evaluating and assessing. If you are distracted by a situation at work, by a project that is overdue or by a conflict with a fellow employee, you will not be fully present at the interview. Critical communication and information will be lost which will affect your later judgment about the candidate.

POINT 3: OPEN THE INTERVIEW PROPERLY.

Begin the interview by observing the basic courtesies. As soon as the candidate is shown in the door, extend your hand, introduce yourself and the panel if you have one. Even if you know the candidate well, a handshake and a warm comment will be appreciated. If you have a panel, please give everybody's titles during the introductions so that the candidate has an understanding of who people are and what role they play. Hearing titles helps candidates during the interview to understand why an interviewer might be focusing on a certain area.

Show the candidate exactly where to sit. No candidate should have to pause to figure that out. Invite the candidate to be comfortable as if the person were a guest in your home. Once you and the candidate are seated, begin by welcoming the candidate to the interview. Impress upon the candidate your delight that he or she is here today and how much you are looking forward to the interview.

Open the interview with some triviality. If you know the candidate, a small joke or a mention of something that has happened in the organization is useful. If the candidate is not known to you, ask if there were any problems parking or if the traffic was bad. It doesn't matter so much what you say just so that the candidate begins to relax and feel at ease.

Do offer the candidate coffee or tea but only if you are having some. In fact, it helps if you already have a cup in hand. Don't let a candidate drink alone. This display of poor manners will make the candidate feel self-conscious.

In other words, do everything that can be done to help the candidate feel comfortable and welcome. This is a nervous time for any candidate and you should go out of your way to help the person to be at ease. Remember that you have a two-fold reason for putting the candidate at ease. First, it demonstrates the professionalism, the sensitivity and the courtesy of your organization and second, comfortable candidates deliver much better interviews. If you can get the candidate to do a good interview, you will have much more information about the candidate which will help you when you choose a candidate to hire.

POINT 4: ASK THE ALREADY PREPARED QUESTIONS.

Sometimes we are tempted in the face-to-face interview to change or to digress significantly from the already prepared questions. Remember to stick to the questions that you have already prepared. There are several reasons for this good practice.

First of all, asking the questions that you already prepared means that you will ask the same questions of each candidate. Asking the same questions gives a common basis for comparison. If your intent is to make a good analysis of each candidate, then you must be able to compare the candidates on the same points. Widely divergent questions will bring out widely divergent responses which will leave you at the end of the day having to compare apples to oranges.

The second reason has to do with the integrity of the interview. A lot of time has already been spent creating questions that were chosen to specifically identify the most important strengths and skills needed for the job. To digress now and ask questions on the fly ruins the integrity of the interview and makes you run the risk of not getting important information from the candidate.

Thirdly, it is your responsibility to make sure that all of the candidates are treated fairly. If one candidate has a set of easy questions and the other one, hard questions, then the candidates are not being treated equally. Everyone deserves a chance to compete on equal footing.

Lastly, and this point is for the public sector, asking different questions can cause the interview to be challenged and thrown out. Candidates who are inside the organization do compare questions afterwards and if they suspect that they were not given equal treatment, they will query the interview process. Even if they are not successful in challenging the interview, it will leave a bad taste in everyone's mouth and may give you a reputation of being unfair. Additionally, the interview process might be held up which may cause you to lose good candidates, who will go elsewhere, while the issue is being resolved.

Of course, this does not mean that you can never diverge from the questions. If further clarification is needed from a candidate regarding something that was said in the interview or if the candidate's background needs to be better understood, naturally other questions can be asked. Sometimes the candidate will have a unique experience that will open up another avenue of discussion. Pursue these opportunities as a lot will be learned about the candidate. Just keep the framework of the interview, with its already prepared questions, intact.

POINT 5: TAKE NOTES.

There are two types of note-taking during an interview.

The first kind of note-taking is interview documentation that will help you later in your evaluation of the candidate. In this type of note-taking, you are recording something that the candidate has said or has done during the interview. These types of notes are usually used as the basis of your comments on a formal evaluation sheet or as part of an informal file to help you remember some significant points about the candidate. Documentation notes are particularly important when a lot of candidates are being interviewed. It is surprising how quickly we can forget what people said when seven or eight different candidates are being seen.

The second type of note-taking is when we want to make a note of something that the candidate has just said so that we can go back to it later in the interview. Sometimes it is not convenient to interrupt the candidate's response just then in order to take a quick note so that the thought is not lost. This type of note-taking is a good habit to get into as it allows you to ask additional questions of the candidate while the candidate is present. Asking the question while the candidate is there is so much better than remembering the point after the candidate has gone and being left to wonder what the candidate would have said.

Whenever notes are taken, be sure to use a certain protocol. Explain to the candidate that notes will be taken from time to time so that the candidate is not distracted by someone writing. Make sure that the candidate cannot read or see your notes and, of course, never doodle. Lastly, have the notepad close to your body so that notes can be taken discreetly. If you have to move significantly everytime that a note is taken, the candidate will be distracted and will be wondering what point was made that was worth keeping.

POINT 6: BE CAREFUL INTERVIEWING ACQUAINTANCES AND COLLEAGUES.

Some of our time as interviewers will be spent interviewing people that we know. This is particularly true in organizations that prefer to promote or transfer from within. When candidates know us and we know the candidates, it adds a sometimes difficult dimension to the interview. When we interview people we know there are some special concerns to consider.

When candidates know us, they tend to exhibit two types of behavior.

First, there is the candidate who becomes a lot more nervous because he or she knows you. The shift in your relationship with the candidate from a colleague, or even a supervisor, to a judge who can award a much-desired job, is a harder shift to make for some than for others. This shift seems to put some candidates under more pressure as they make a sudden mental transition seeing you in a different role. The other pressure for these candidates comes as a result of their belief, not mistakenly, that there is something more that is at stake. In this case, these candidates are determined to have you think well of them even if they don't get the job. These candidates are overly preoccupied with their reputation and their standing in your eyes—neither of which they want to damage during the interview process.

The other type of behavior is from candidates who are too much at ease. Since they know you and perhaps the other panelists, they feel that their relationship with you as well as their already established reputation will carry them through the interview. Sometimes, these candidates do not prepare adequately or use too casual a demeanour during the interview. In this case, they have permitted their day to day relationship with you to have influenced their thinking about the interview. Instead of seeing the interview as a professional, competitive process, they see it as a friendly chat between established colleagues.

The fact is that both responses are inappropriate and if you see candidates going down either of these paths, you have to help them so that they do not hurt their interview. With nervous candidates, try to put them at their ease by treating them with the friendly approach that is used every day. With candidates who are too casual, take on a more formal tone to get them to smarten up. With the latter, however, be prepared to not succeed unless the candidate is quite sensitive to the environment. Moreover, be prepared to be criticized afterwards for being too formal in the interview.

Now, you might say to yourself, if these candidates are making these type of judgment errors, are they the candidates that I would want in the job? I consider these behaviorial problems to be relatively minor and very common and they are usually not a reflection of the person's behavior on the job.

Another area of concern, however, is your own behavior. You must watch out for three problem areas when you interview people you know. First, make sure that you are not too casual in case the interview becomes sloppy and sends a message to the candidate that the interview is not important. Second, don't let a candidate that you know well off the hook when difficult questions are being asked in the interview. Often we are reluctant to put people whom we know and like into difficult situations. While our inclination might be either to help the candidate through the questions or to let them slide on the tougher questions, we cannot jeopardize the quality of the interview. It isn't fair to the candidates who we don't know who have to go through the full process and it isn't fair to the candidates that we do know because they may never have a chance to show what they can do.

Lastly, it is very easy when we are interviewing someone that we know to start discussing the business or the gossip of the organization. While some of that is fine for the warm-up as well as the conclusion of the interview, too much will erode the time that you should be spending trying to understand the candidate's skills and abilities. Just watch out for this very common problem.

POINT 7: DON'T TELL ABOUT THE JOB FIRST.

Many times we have the impulse to begin the interview by telling the candidate about the job. However, this is an impulse that must be checked. We must remember that we are there to learn about the candidate and not to hear ourselves talk. What we need to know is what the candidate thinks about the job. If we give a great deal of information first about our priorities for the job, our goals and our interests, any smart candidate is going to shape his or her answers to fit our already stated expectations. Therefore, let the candidate speak first and tell you what the candidate knows about the job, its priorities and its goals.

Another reason not to tell about the job first is that you might may want to find out how much homework a candidate has done. A candidate's research about the job and the organization can give you some indication as to the level of the candidate's motivation for the job because candidates that have done their homework probably have a greater interest in the position. If you tell a lot about the job at the beginning of the interview, it will be unclear to you how much the candidate already knows or how much has just been picked up from your speech.

A word of caution. Sometimes candidates will ask at the end of the interview about the job and its goals and priorities. This is a perfectly acceptable time for you to talk about the job but it must be done in a proper fashion. Do not make the candidate feel by your description of the job that he or she was way off in their answers in the interview. Be sensitive to what the candidate said during the interview. That is not a time to make the candidate feel bad either unintentionally or otherwise. Another pitfall to beware of can sometimes arise as a result of your description of the job. A candidate will feel that he or she has answered some questions inappropriately. Such candidates may attempt to amend their responses. You must gently stop this impulse. After all, you don't want to conduct a second interview.

POINT 8: BE PROMPT.

Sometimes delays are unavoidable in an interview day. For example, there may have been an emergency or the candidates, and sometimes the panelists, may have been more talkative than was expected. There are many circumstances that can affect even the best planned of days. However, as much as possible, be prompt when interviewing candidates. There is nothing worse than a candidate waiting and waiting for an interview. This type of wait increases the candidate's anxiety and makes the organization look unprofessional.

Be particularly careful around the lunch hour. It is unacceptable to have a candidate observing you strolling back from a long lunch while the candidate has been cooling his or her heels.

POINT 9: WATCH BOTH VOICE TONE AND BODY LANGUAGE.

As closely as you are watching the candidate, so also is the candidate watching you. Consciously or subconsciously, your voice tone and body language are constantly giving subtle cues to the candidate as to your feelings about the interview. You should watch your voice tone and body language to ensure that both convey interest, professionalism and ease.

If your tone and manner are too brusque, the candidate will be intimidated. If you look bored or your voice lacks interest, the candidate will give up trying. If you look at the clock, the candidate will rush. Therefore, lean back in a relaxed, but not overly-relaxed manner, and nod your head to show that you are listening, but not necessarily agreeing. Also, be sure to look, really look, at the candidate. Eyes that are drifting out the window or to papers on the desk or down at your hands are a clear indication to the candidate that you are not fully engaged in the interview. It must be conveyed to the candidate that you are one hundred percent involved.

Are there reasons why we watch both our voice tone and body language? First, this demonstrates the professionalism and courtesy of the interview and second, it allows candidates to give much better interviews once they are assured that we are really interested in them. It is in our best interests to get candidates to give really good interviews so that we can fully judge the person's ability.

POINT 10: CONTROL THE INTERVIEW.

If necessary, you must control the interview. Most of the time controlling the interview will not be needed as candidates usually exhibit the correct behavior and know where to draw the line between appropriate and inappropriate behavior. However, sometimes you will get a candidate who exhibits inappropriate behavior that must be controlled. Let's take a look at what some of those behaviors are.

The most likely inappropriate behavior will be the overly talkative candidate. The overly talkative candidate goes on and on, giving an extreme amount of detail or digressing into other areas. Often, this type of candidate answers questions not yet asked or never intended to be asked. Our response is often boredom and a sincere desire to be elsewhere. If you have a candidate who rambles on an on, say this as soon as the candidate draws breath "thank you for your response. I have enough information for now. Let's move onto the next question." Most candidates will get the message but, if not, just keep repeating this phrase until you can close the interview. You must be very assertive in order to control the talkative candidate. Don't feel bad about behaving in what may seem to be a rude fashion to you. Remember that people with this type of problem have been deeply anxious and insecure all their lives. No interviewer is going to control the talkative behavior of a lifetime without being very firm in the interview.

One more tip in dealing with the talkative candidate is for you to watch your own behavior. Do not digress in these interviews either. Just ask the basic questions and go no further in clarifying the candidate's background or experience. There is no point in investing more time on such candidates. After all, if the candidate is this way in the interview, imagine the person on the job!

Next, you might encounter a candidate who is very aggressive or hostile. This is difficult to handle. If this happens, relax, use your most professional voice and quiet their demeanour. Close the interview as soon as possible and show the candidate out. Be calm but firm. Do nothing that will disturb or distress the candidate further nor anything that will give the candidate any indication that everything is other than just fine. If the candidate seems dangerous to you personally, calmly excuse yourself by faking a cough or feeling ill or some other strategy so that you can leave the room. Get help immediately. No person has to put up with that type of behavior.

If you do encounter such a candidate, be sure to keep a record of what has occured. This type of person might resurface later and you want to make sure that you have all of the necessary documentation in the event of any legal issues.

Sometimes a person's aggression will take the form of dominance. In this case, the candidate will attempt to control the interview. This candidate might talk at length, try to ask an inappropriate number of questions, or have a condescending manner. I have had candidates who had problems with dominance express surprise at my gender and my age, when I was younger. You should handle such candidates much as you would the talkative candidate. Be firm both in cutting off the conversation and in closing the interview as soon as possible. Again, you need to be very assertive in these circumstances without, of course, creating a conflict situation which this type of personality easily gets into.

Sometimes, candidates might become emotionally distraught or show some other sign of instability. There is little to be done for such candidates except to treat them kindly, close the interview early and make sure that they are stable enough to go home.

Sometimes candidates will bring relatives with them to the interview. This is not acceptable and you should ask the relative, in a kindly fashion, to wait outside.

Don't consider the candidate's nervousness in the interview as inappropriate behavior. Nervousness is typical for all but the most experienced of candidates. Just help a nervous candidate to relax by kind treatment and humour. Of course, if the nervousness is inappropriate for the level of the position that is vacant, you would want to consider if the candidate is really ready for that job.

POINT 11: PROTECT CANDIDATES FROM YOUR BIASES.

It is very important that we protect candidates from our personal biases and prejudices. The interview is a process that should be based not on prejudice but on rationality.

Unfortunately, we are only human after all. There is not a person on this earth that does not have prejudices. The creation of prejudices begins carelessly in early childhood. By the time that we are adults, we accept many prejudices as if they are fact. However, for us to be skillful interviewers, we must recognize what prejudices we do have and the irrational nature of those prejudices. Importantly, we must recognize that we have the mental discipline to not act upon our deep-seated prejudices in the interview process. Therefore, if you know that you do not like a certain type of person or behavior, you must articulate those feelings to yourself and be prepared to go beyond them to a more rational place. Your focus should not be on what your prejudice is saying but rather on what the candidate is saying.

Now, sometimes we as interviewers act out our prejudices when we encounter a candidate who embodies the race, national heritage, body type, gender, and so forth that we know we don't like. Let's look at some of the behavior that we need to control in ourselves.

First and foremost, watch your tone of voice. Candidates can easily pick up on a tone that is patronizing, sarcastic, or demeaning. Second, be careful not to ask questions that are sneaky or loaded or put words in the mouth of the candidate so that you hear what you want to hear not what the candidate wants to say. Third, watch your language. Using terms such as "girl" to a grown woman and other archaic expressions reveals a total lack of awareness and sensitivity. Fourth, be aware of your response to people with accents. If you have a disgusted look on your face or if you speak in an exaggeratedly slow manner, the candidate will be well aware of what you are doing. Lastly, watch what you wear to the interview. Certain kinds of pins and symbols might be offensive to a candidate and will reveal your prejudices.

The point is to be fair to the candidate and to be fair to yourself. Don't let your silly prejudices cause you to lose a great candidate.

POINT 12: AVOID THE HALO EFFECT.

The halo effect refers to a tendency by interviewers to assume that candidates who are likeable must also be very good at their jobs. In other words, when we enjoy someone's personality, we also assume that the person is smart, kind, and capable. This explains how sometimes people with terrific personalities, but marginal abilities, get jobs, and keep them, and even get promoted.

You must learn to be very aware of the emergence of feelings of liking for the candidate in the interview. No person is perfect. Check out your feelings during the interview so that your prejudice for a candidate's personality does not blind you to the person's abilities.

How do we do this? Say for example, as the interview progresses, that you begin to form a completely positive view of the candidate. At that point of awareness, start probing more deeply. Listen beyond the personality into the structure and the depth of the answers. Do the answers just sound good or are they really good? Challenging your own feelings during the interview will give you a more balanced view of the candidate and a deeper understanding of the candidate's abilities. It will also give you some security that you have not been blinded just by a charming personality but instead have found a candidate with both personality and ability.

POINT 13: DON'T OVERSELL THE POSITION.

Once in awhile, we will be interviewing a candidate and have a strong feeling that the candidate is exactly right for us. Since no one wants such a candidate to get away, there is a tendency to start to oversell the position during the interview.

When we really want a candidate, it is only natural for us to start to make the job as attractive as possible in order to hold the candidate's interest. However, you must be careful to present at all times a realistic picture of the position. Do not make the job more than it is because then the candidate will have false expectations and eventually disappointment on the job. Remember, we must always be looking for a match between a candidate and the job. If either is false, then the match will not be good.

When the candidate asks about the job, even if the candidate looks great, just state plainly what the job entails. Be honest about the position's pros and cons. This is only fair to the candidate and to the organization who wants a candidate who understands what the job is really about.

Lastly, there is little point in pitching a job when you have not seen all of the candidates and certainly no references have been checked. Therefore, just take it easy and let the interview flow.

POINT 14: GIVE THE CANDIDATE TIME TO RESPOND.

Sometimes when a question is asked that may be beyond the range of experience of the candidate or particularly complicated, the candidate will fall silent while thinking of a response. That silence is awkward and you must watch your own behavior during this time.

The first inappropriate behavior that you might be tempted to employ is to rush in and let the candidate off the hook by saying something like "don't worry about that question, let's go to the next one". Since we have all been in the place of the candidate, it is only natural that we have compassion for that person and a desire to rescue him or her from a difficult situation. However, the candidate must respond to the questions. After all, if the candidate is not expected to answer all the questions, how will you know whether or not this person had the necessary skills for the job. Moreover, even if you think you are helping the candidate by bypassing the question, actually you are hurting the candidate who either will worry about not being able to answer a question or will not have a chance to demonstrate ability in that area.

Instead, when the awkward silence occurs, give the candidate space. If you see that the candidate is uncomfortable say, "it's allright, take a few minutes to think". After that has been said, relax and wait for a response. Of course, be sure during this silence not to start up a conversation with the panel if you have one.

The other inappropriate behavior on your part is to rush a candidate who clearly needs more time for thought. This will guarantee that the candidate will give wrong, incomplete or strange answers. Then, once a candidate feels that one answer was poorly done, the responses that follow may also deteriorate because the candidate's nervousness has increased and the candidate's mind might be preoccupied on what could have been said. There is no need to rush candidates. Remember, this is an interview, not a thoroughbred race.

Once in awhile, you will encounter a candidate who genuinely cannot answer a question. First, make sure that the candidate really is stuck. The candidate will say something like "I'm sorry, I just cannot think of an answer." You can give the candidate more time or ask the question in a different way. Depending upon the question, you could also pull it apart so that the candidate might be able to reflect on some aspect of it. If the candidate is still in trouble, just move the interview on without comment. Candidates fail to answer questions sometimes because of suffering from really bad nerves and sometimes as a result of a complete lack of experience in the area of the question. Make sure that you note later what question the candidate could not answer as the failure to answer a question is critical information in the evaluation process.

POINT 15: BE CAREFUL WITH RESPONSES.

One of the awkward points in an interview is when the candidate has finished speaking but the next question has not yet been asked. Often we feel the need to acknowledge the candidate's answer in some way so we say things such as "very good . . . what a great answer . . . oh, really . . . thank you". While such banalties are not bad in and of themselves, be careful to not reinforce the candidate one way or the other by making comments that may seem to be approving or disapproving of the answers. What is important in the interview is searching out what the candidate truly thinks and feels. If you are accidentally reinforcing a candidate one way or the other through these offhanded comments, you may begin to skew the candidate's responses and get a false picture of the candidate.

If you cannot control yourself from giving responses, then substitute those comments by using transition sentences which will link what the candidate has said to the next question. So instead of saying "what an interesting point" say something like "earlier on, you mentioned that you had experience in customer service, our next question is about a customer service problem . . . " However, since not every comment makes a transition, just make every effort to go onto the next question without comment.

POINT 16: LET THE APPLICANT TALK.

Letting the applicant talk means that you listen. One of the most common faults of inexperienced interviewers is that they feel that they need to "keep the ball rolling". However, candidates will do plenty of talking if they are given a chance. A candidate should do at least eighty percent of the talking in an interview. After all, you are there to find out how the candidate thinks and feels. You already know how you think and feel.

Another advantage of letting a candidate talk is that he or she will often give unsolicited comments which can be very useful in evaluation.

Let the interview be a showcase for the candidate's talents and abilities not a forum for yourself.

POINT 17: DON'T BE NERVOUS.

Sometimes interviewers will be more nervous than the candidates. An inexperienced interviewer might be too worried about the interview process going well, be very shy, or be intimidated by the candidates, the other panelists, or by the interview process.

It is hard to say this any other way but don't be nervous. For one thing, the person who is conducting the interview holds all the cards. For another, if you are nervous, the candidates will figure that out quickly and will exhibit an interesting range of reactions. Some candidates that are less mature will either become nervous themselves, or will start to dominate the interview or will patronize you. It will then be difficult for you to control the interview and get the information that you need. A more sophisticated candidate will work with you and will ignore your nervousness. However, every candidate certainly will be puzzled by your nervous behavior initially. This could start off the interview with a less than perfect tone.

Probably the worst thing about being nervous, apart from the embarrassment, is that you will not listen as effectively as is necessary and will miss out on the important things that candidate is saying.

Most of the time we grow out of nervousness after a little experience. However if you find yourself continuing to be nervous, you do need to determine what it is about this environment that intimidates you.

POINT 18: BE FLEXIBLE WITH THE QUESTIONS.

Just because the questions have been numbered one through ten does not mean that they have to be asked that way. Be flexible with the questions. Let the interview have more flow with the questions being asked spontaneously in a different order and by different people if you have a panel. There might be a tiny amount of humorous chaos since there will be no order to the questions but it will be more enjoyable for everyone and the interview will take on a more conversational tone. Moreover, these small changes will keep interest up when there are a lot of candidates to be seen that day. There is nothing more dreary than eight hours of interviewing with no variation.

There are two other possible approaches to being flexible on the questions. These two approaches are not often used but you may wish to try them out. The first is to tell the candidate at the start of the interview what all the questions are. This relaxes the candidate who hears the questions first and realizes that nothing too difficult is looming. It also allows the candidate to start thinking about the questions. With this technique, after you have told the candidate about the questions, you should begin by asking the routine questions about the candidate's background . Answering the easier questions first allows the candidate to begin formulating responses to the upcoming questions in the background of his or her mind.

The second technique is to give the candidate the questions written out on a piece of paper. With this approach, the candidate can scan the questions before you begin asking. As with the technique above, it also has the desired effect of calming the candidate down. Its drawback occurs when the the candidate is too print-oriented and becomes more attentive to what is written and less to what is said. Of course, that behavior is also information for you.

I should note that these two techniques can backfire. If a candidate sees in advance questions that are hard, he or she may become too worried about what is to come and may stumble on other questions that could have been answered perfectly well because of being preoccupied with the upcoming questions. For this reason, you may want to use these two techniques on more experienced candidates.

POINT 19: REPEAT QUESTIONS IF NECESSARY.

It is not a disgrace if the candidate did not understand the question the first time. There are several reasons for this. Sometimes candidates just miss a crucial word. Sometimes candidates are nervous which reduces listening effectiveness. Sometimes, they just did not understand the question and so you may need not only to repeat the question but also to clarify it. It may also be that the candidate is speaking English as a second language. The candidate may even have a slight hearing disability. There are many reasons for people to ask for a question to be repeated so just repeat it and clarify it without passing judgment on the candidate's ability. Of course, if the candidate asks for every question to be repeated, then there is a problem with the candidate.

Sometimes a candidate will not hear the question correctly but will proceed to answer what the candidate thought the question was and, then, realize that something is wrong and ask you "am I answering your question?" In this case, simply clarify for the candidate what the question was. Of course, if you want to be very diplomatic, you can find something in the candidate's response to pick up on to clarify the question. Expressions such as "given what you have just said" or "in addition to what you have just said, if you would like to tell us now about . . . " all make the candidate feel good. There is certainly something to be respected about candidates who know that they are going down the wrong path and correct themselves.

POINT 20: BE FAIR TO PEOPLE WITH DISABILITIES.

Those of us without serious physical disabilities and without any training or exposure to people who do have disabilities are often at a loss when we interview a candidate with a physical limitation. Let's look at six areas in particular that may occur in the interview.

First of all, when a candidate comes through our doors with a disability, there is a tendency to be overly solicitous, overly mannered, or easier on the candidate. Remember that the candidate is there for the same reason everyone else is—to get a job. Look at the candidate's ability and talents just as you are doing in all the other interviews. Don't patronize this candidate.

Second is the challenge that we face when a candidate has a serious speech difficulty. Relax and listen carefully. Ask the candidate to repeat when needed or to write on paper anything that you are not getting. Remember that this candidate is accustomed to people having problems. Just take your time with the candidate.

Third, many of us do not know how to behave around a candidate who has an interpreter. A candidate might bring an interpreter when the candidate is unable to speak, or whose speech is difficult to follow or who has a hearing disability. The problem for most of us is that we do not know where to look—do we look at the candidate or at the interpreter? The answer is—you look at the candidate with occasional glances for clarification and courtesy to the interpreter. Most of us are so trained in this society for our eyes to follow wherever speech is that we feel it is rude to not concentrate on the interpreter. However, your conversation is with the candidate. The interpreter, no disrespect intended, is a medium of communication for the candidate.

The fourth issue occurs when the candidate has a physical disability that brings unusual or frequent physical movement that may surprise you. Don't focus on this or you will not be able to really listen to what the candidate has to say. Just ignore the movement although don't be pointed about ignoring it.

Fifth, shaking hands with a person with certain physical disabilities is often uncertain for people unaccustomed to dealing with disabled persons. Begin to make the gesture of handshaking, depending upon what disability you see, and follow the candidate's lead as to how to go about that.

Remember not to be awkward. Persons with disabilities have learned long ago to live with these issues.

Finally, persons who are visually impaired may need some special assistance if they do not have anyone with them. After introducing yourself, ask the candidate if you may show him or her to the chair. Take the candidate lightly by the arm and direct him or her towards the chair. Never grab or touch the candidate without permission. People who are visually impaired can explain very well to you what their needs are.

Just try to be sensitive and treat the candidate with a disability with the same courtesy as you would anyone else.

POINT 21: DISCERN THE TRUTH OF THE RESPONSES.

Once in awhile when we are interviewing candidates, we get a distinct feeling that the candidate is lying to us. There may be some discrepancy in the responses, the experiences, the educational achievements, or some body language that indicates that the candidate is being less than truthful. If this occurs, just probe the issue more fully by asking, tactfully, if the candidate would clarify a couple of the points that you are not understanding fully. This will either clear up the matter or give you more indication that the candidate may be lying. You owe it to yourself and to the candidate to resolve your suspicions if you can. It may be just a matter of clarification. However, if you are still suspicious after the clarification, let it go—this will not be the candidate for you.

Do be careful when you think that the candidate's body language is revealing that the candidate is lying. Body language can be very misleading particularly when communicating across cultures. Unfortunately, all we have to go on is our instincts at that moment. So if you think that the body language is telling you something, keep observing and assessing while the candidate is speaking. Once again, if you still remain suspicious, this is not the candidate for you.

POINT 22: GIVE THE CANDIDATE TIME TO ASK QUESTIONS.

For most candidates, changing jobs is a major decision in which a lot is at stake. Give the candidate time to ask questions about the job. If a candidate does not receive the clarification needed regarding certain issues, he or she may be turned off from the job and you might lose a good candidate.

Answer all of the candidate's questions in a straight-forward fashion without being patronizing and without over-elaboration. Remember not to give inside gossip or to say anything that would be damaging to the image of your organization.

Make note of what type of questions the candidate is asking. The questions are an indication of the candidate's direction, priorities, and interests. Ascertain also if the questions are appropriate to the level of the candidate. This will indicate to you if the candidate sees the job in the proper perspective. Pay attention because the candidate's questions can give you important information.

Once in awhile, we encounter a candidate who is asking an unreasonable amount of questions or who is asking questions in detail about salary and benefits even though the job has not yet been offered. In the first case, just politely bring the interview to a close. In the second case, inform the candidate in as polite a manner as possible that such information can be discussed at a later time if the candidate is chosen. You may also want to send this person for further information to the Personnel Office if you have one.

Finally, let the candidate have time to say a few words. Ask the candidate if there is anything that he or she would like to add that would help you to evaluate them as a candidate. The candidate's summation is also information for you.

POINT 23: DON'T LET CANDIDATES KNOW HOW THEY DID.

Sometimes candidates will ask, at the close of the interview, how they did. Respond in a polite fashion but give no feedback at this time. There is a good reason for this—there is no feedback to give. After all, some of the candidates may not have been seen, evaluations have not been done and references have not been checked. Therefore, do not respond negatively or affirmatively to candidates. Do not give them false hope or give them any promises before the complete process of the interview is over. Needless to say, absolutely no candidate is ever offered a job on the spot. Instead, say something like "we really enjoyed meeting you and we appreciate the time that you have given". This is enough of a pleasantry and it closes the discussion.

POINT 24: CLOSE THE INTERVIEW PROPERLY.

The close of the interview again reveals the professionalism of the interviewer. Close the interview in this sequence. First, if you have a panel, ask everyone if they have any more questions or comments. Second, inform the candidate when the final decision about the position will be made. Third, thank the candidate, saying what a pleasure it was to have this interview. Fourth, shake hands all around. Fifth, show the candidate to the door as you would a guest in your house.

Observing the courtesies up to the very last moment of the interview leaves a very good impression in the candidate's mind regardless of whether or not the candidate was successful.

POINT 25: GATHER UP ALL FILES.

Remember that the interview is a confidential process. At the close of each interview and the interview day, gather up all your files and keep them in a safe place. You do not want your interview questions or your personal notes on the candidates seen by anyone but you.

CONCLUSION

When all is said and done, you have only a few moments in time to assess a candidate's talents, abilities, and aptitude. You must make the most of this time in order to determine who is the best candidate. Conducting the interview properly is the most critical step towards hiring the best candidate for the job.

CONDUCTING THE INTERVIEW

QUICK CHECK

Point 1: Review the application, resume and questions.

- Do you know the candidate's background?
- Have you reviewed the questions again?
- Are the papers in a convenient location?

Point 2: Relax and concentrate.

- Are you completely engaged in the interview?
- Is your mind free of other concerns?

Point 3: Open the interview properly.

- Has the candidate been welcomed properly?
- Has the interview begun with some pleasantries?
- Was everyone introduced?

Point 4: Ask the already prepared questions.

- Is there a common basis for comparison for the candidates?
- Are the candidates being treated fairly?
- Is the integrity of the interview being preserved?

Point 5: Take notes.

- Has the candidate been informed that notes will be taken?
- Are the candidate's comments being documented?
- Are you making side notes as reminders?
- Is a disturbance being created with note-taking?

Point 6: Be careful interviewing acquaintances and colleagues.

- Do you need to help the nervous candidate?
- Is the candidate too much at ease?
- Is your own behavior appropriate?

Point 7: Don't tell about the job first.

- Has the candidate had a chance to speak first about the job?
- Is it known how much homework the candidate has done for the job?

Point 8: Be prompt.

- Are the interviews on time?
- Are you back from lunch in a timely fashion?

Point 9: Watch both voice tone and body language.

- Does your voice and body convey professionalism and ease?
- Do you look bored or intimidating?

Point 10: Control the interview.

- Have you been assertive enough with the talkative candidate?
- Have you been assertive enough with the dominant or hostile candidate?
- Has the candidate's normal nervousness been disregarded?

Point 11: Protect candidates from your biases.

- Do you know your own prejudices?
- Have you avoided behavior that shows biases?
- Are you using modern and sensitive language?
- Have any symbols or pins that might be offensive to the candidate been avoided?

Point 12: Avoid the halo effect.

- Are you aware of your feelings about the candidate during the interview?
- Have you looked for a balanced perspective of the candidate?
- Has the "halo effect" been avoided?

Point 13: Don't oversell the position.

- Has the job been oversold?
- Are you too eager to employ this candidate?
- Are you being honest with the candidate about the job?

Point 14: Give the candidate time to respond.

- Did the candidate have time to think?
- Did the candidate respond to all the questions?
- How has the candidate who cannot answer a question been evaluated?
- Did you rush the candidate?

Point 15: Be careful with responses.

- Have you avoided making inappropriate responses to the candidate after answer?
- Has the candidate's response been tied to the next question?
- Are the responses neutral?

Point 16: Let the applicant talk.

- Is the candidate during 80% of the talking? Is the candidate allowed to give unsolicited information?
- Has the interview been a showcase for the candidate?

Point 17: Don't be nervous.

- Has nervousness on your part been controlled?
- Has listening effectiveness been reduced by nervousness?
- Do you understand why you are nervous?

Point 18: Be flexible with the questions.

- Is the question sequence too rigid?
- Can different people ask different questions?
- Does the interview have variety?
- Have you considered showing the candidate the questions at the beginning?

Point 19: Repeat questions if necessary.

- Are you repeating the questions when the candidate asks?
- Is the candidate being judged harshly because questions were repeated?
- Is the candidate speaking the same language as a primary language?

- Do you have an accent that the candidate has trouble following?
- Are the questions being repeated in a tactful manner?

Point 20: Be fair to people with disabilities.

- Have you been overly solicitous?
- Are you listening directly to the candidate?
- Have you assisted people with special disabilities?
- Are you treating the candidate as you would any candidate?

Point 21: Discern the truth of the responses.

- Do you think that the candidate might be lying?
- Have you probed the issues that need clarification more fully?
- Have you assessed the body language closely to make sure that you are not being misled?

Point 22: Give the candidate time to ask questions.

- Have candidates been allowed to ask their questions?
- Are the questions being answered in a straight-forward and honest fashion?
- Has a note been made of what the candidates are asking?
- Have candidates been allowed a chance to add information at the end of the interview?
- Has the overly talkative candidate been re-directed?

Point 23: Don't let candidates know how they did.

- Were candidates who asked about their interview given a neutral response?
- Did you avoid any statement that seemed like a promise to the candidate?

Point 24: Close the interview properly.

- Was everyone asked if they were finished?
- Did everyone shake hands and thank the candidate?
- Was the candidate escorted to the door?
- Was the candidate left with an image of professionalism and courtesy?

Point 25: Gather up all files.

- Have you kept all the interview files in a confidential place?

5 EXTENDING THE INTERVIEW PROCESS

POINTS TO REMEMBER

Point 1: Take the candidate to lunch.
Point 2: Ask the candidate to make a speech.
Point 3: Role-play with the candidate.
Point 4: Conduct an in-basket exam.
Point 5: Take the candidate on a tour.
Point 6: Give the candidate time alone.
Point 7: Manage the telephone interview.

EXTENDING THE INTERVIEW PROCESS

In some cases, due to the level or complexity of a position or because of its impact upon the organization, we want to have as much opportunity as possible to evaluate candidates. If this is the case, consider extending the face-to-face interview with supplemental processes which can provide you with increased knowledge and, sometimes, with a different perspective on the candidate. This added information gives you another chance to see if the candidate will suit the job. Now, there are many kinds of supplemental processes including oral presentations, in-basket tests, or role-playing. Each type of process has certain issues and problems of which you should be aware. Let's take a look now at how to extend the interview process.

POINT 1: TAKE THE CANDIDATE TO LUNCH.

Taking a candidate to lunch, particularly one that is interviewing for most of the day with the organization, may seem just like a basic courtesy. However, the over-the-lunch interview is a tried and true method of evaluating the candidate in a different setting other than the office.

Why is the luncheon interview valuable? At lunchtime, you can see how the candidate interacts in a social setting with strangers. Over lunch, you can observe the candidate's social skills, conversational abilities and manners. These aspects of a candidate are particularly important if the job is at a high enough level to be performing many social or public functions. But at any level, you will want to see how the candidate interacts with people in a more casual environment. Candidates often let their guard down a little over lunch and let you see their truer personality.

Let's look at how to manage the lunch time interview. First of all, take care of the logistics ahead of time. Have all the luncheon arrangements made before the candidate arrives. Plan in advance which restaurant to attend, how to get there, who goes in what car, and how to pay for lunch. The candidate should not overhear any of the logistics of the lunch. Nor should the candidate be standing around while you and your colleagues decide where to go. This indecisiveness or lack of organization may reflect poorly upon you. This is an opportunity to demonstrate the organization's professionalism. Additionally, disorganization will waste time during what may be a crowded interview day.

Have some consideration for the candidate about where you go to lunch. Barbecue houses, corn on the cob, excessively spicy or unusual foods are difficult to handle and can make for an uncomfortable lunch. Do find out if the candidate has any dietary restrictions.

Think through in advance whether or not to have alcohol at lunch. Generally, it is better to avoid it as it will reduce your effectiveness, unless the candidate will be handling a lot of social events on the job and you want to see how the candidate handles drinking. Of course, you should make sure that everyone else at lunch handles liquor well also. After all, you do not want to loose a candidate because of the staff's behavior with alcohol.

Think through who is going to lunch with you and the candidate. Anyone who will be interacting extensively with the candidate should go. Consider also inviting the person who handles personnel matters. Keep it small—no more than three or four. More people than that and the candidate will get lost in the crowd. A large group can easily carry a conversation and distract you so if you want to see the candidate's conversational and social skills, then the luncheon should not be crowded with people. The spotlight should remain on the candidate.

Remind yourself and any staff accompanying you that the candidate is still being interviewed and that the same rules of interviewing still apply. Just because everyone is at lunch does not mean that the candidate can be asked illegal questions. Questions about home life, child care, and national origin are just as inappropriate here as they are in the office setting.

Encourage the candidate to talk and observe if the candidate keeps the conversation ball rolling. Make a mental note of what questions the candidate asks. See if there are hobbies, skills, or sports that would make the candidate fit in with the work group. Ascertain the candidate's humour and manners. Ask yourself if you are enjoying having lunch with this person. The challenge is to keep the lunch casual while still learning important things about the candidate. Remember when you get back to the office to jot down your thoughts. The impressions you have gained during lunch will be very important when you are making your decision about the candidate.

Two last thoughts. Be sure to let the candidate have a chance to eat. Sometimes we ply candidates with so many questions during lunch that they have only gotten one bite. This is particularly unfair if they have a long day still ahead. Second, remember that you and the people with you are also being observed by the candidate. There is always a tendency with a small group who work together to talk shop. Inside gossip about fellow workers, sarcastic remarks about the organization, or too much in-crowd talk can turn off a good candidate. Remember that the candidate is a guest and should be treated accordingly.

POINT 2: ASK THE CANDIDATE TO MAKE A SPEECH.

If the job calls for a lot of public speaking, consider asking the candidates to make a speech. It is a good way to evaluate their poise, the logic of their thought, their understanding of their work, and their personality.

If you want to have candidates make a speech, decide first of all if you want to notify them in advance or on the day of the interview that a speech will be required.

Let's look first at informing candidates in advance of the interview day that they will be asked to make a speech. Informing candidates in advance gives them time to prepare notes and time to prepare mentally. The advantage of informing candidates in advance is that you can see what their work is like when there has been a chance to prepare. Prepared work is usually richer in thought and more logical in presentation.

At what point should you let the candidates know that they will be giving a speech? Inform candidates that they will be required to give a speech when you are giving them general information about the interview day and time. Then mail out the information about the speech so that they have about a week to prepare. Don't give them weeks to work on the speech as they will work on it to a point where it will be overkill. Also, please do not give the speech information to them the night before the interview. They are nervous enough anyway and need a good night's sleep.

The second approach is to give candidates no advance notice but to let them know, when they are at the interview site, that they will be making a presentation that day. The advantage of not giving advance notice is that you will be able to see how well the candidates can speak on professional or organizational issues without much forethought. The ability of a candidate to speak at the drop of a hat will reveal their level of professional development. People who take their profession seriously usually do not have much trouble speaking about it with short notice.

Giving candidates no advance notice will also tell you how well they think on their feet and how well they perform under stress. Watch for the reaction of the candidates when they have been informed that they will speak. Is it panic, amusement, interest, or resignation that appears on their faces? Their reaction will give you an idea of how they will react on the job when something sudden occurs.

Usually about fifteen to thirty minutes at the most is adequate for a candidate to prepare for a speech. More than that and the speech will get too long. Less than that and it may be unnecessarily stressful for the candidate.

Be sure to provide a private place in which a candidate can work on the speech. The space should have a computer or, at least, all writing materials that may be needed.

However, whether you are giving candidates a week or a few minutes to prepare will depend upon whether you want to test their ability to speak by giving them preparation time for an organized, more developed speech or whether you want to test their ability to think on their feet by giving them only a few minutes to prepare.

No matter which way you go, it will be clearer and easier for the candidates if you give them written instructions about the speech. Thus, the candidates will all have the same information and nothing will be forgotten by you or the candidates. The instructions should give information about the time frame for speaking, the topic, the imaginary situation if any, the setting and the audience.

First of all, give them a time frame in which to speak. Anywhere from five to fifteen minutes usually works best. In less than five minutes, not much can be said. If you allow more than fifteen minutes, then you will become very bored listening to a number of candidates all day long. Once boredom sets in, listening stops. Once listening stops, the whole purpose of having the candidates prepare a speech is spoiled.

Do give the candidates the topic of their speech. Not only does this provide some focus for them but it also gives you a basis for comparison. It is much easier to compare abilities and philosophies if all the candidates are speaking, for example, about customer service rather than one speaking about customer service, another about finance and a third talking about planning.

While giving candidates the topic of their speech, let them know if there is an imaginary situation that goes with it. For example, do you want them to pretend that they are making a presentation before the Chamber of Commerce? Before a major client? Before the CEO? Identifying imaginary situations will give the candidates some idea of how to develop their speech.

Let the candidates know something about the setting in which they will be speaking. Is it a conference room? A small auditorium? Physical space affects the mode of presentation so it will help candidates if they have some idea in advance.

Give the candidates some idea of the size of the audience that will be listening to their speech. Will it just be you? You and the panel? You and several staff? Again, this will help candidates to shape the speech appropriately.

Do consider whether or not the candidates should be videotaped during the speech. Videotaping should only be done if you want someone else who did not see the candidates to view the tape or if you really want to evaluate the speeches in more detail later on. Videotaping does create more stress for the candidate and, of course, is more work and expense for the organization. Therefore, only use it when you really need it.

When the speech is being evaluated, look first of all for the style of presentation. Was the candidate an interesting speaker? Is the speech animated and lively? Is is humorous? What about the content? Is it substantial? Does it have logic and common sense? Then, look at the candidate's imagination. Are routine topics presented in a different way? Does the speech capture the imagination? Does it have vision? Finally, was the candidate capable of reaching out to the audience or did the speech leave everyone cold?

Once again, be sure to take notes on your impressions of the candidates so that the notes can be used in later evaluations of the candidates.

POINT 3: ROLE PLAY WITH THE CANDIDATE.

Role-playing refers to a process in which the candidates simulate a particular experience which occurs in the work environment. For the moment in time in which they are role-playing, candidates act as if they were at work in true to life situations. The purpose of role-playing is to see how well candidates really perform on the job. Role-playing also demonstrates how well candidates work under stress as all role-playing is quite stressful.

You must have good reasons to have role-playing as a supplemental process because role-playing is costly and time-consuming to produce. Therefore, only use role-playing in "mission critical" positions, that is, with higher level staff or with staff in pivotal jobs that have a lot of impact on your organization.

Let's look now at how to set-up a role playing exercise.

First of all, the imaginary situation must be created. Like the interview questions, this situation should be based on the skills needed for the job. For example, if the job calls for someone who can handle personnel problems then you may want to set up a role play in which there is a personnel problem. If the job is in customer service, you might want to set up a role play in which there is an angry customer who did not receive his shipments. Other role play ideas might include a public relations problem, a group of staff angry over a manager's decision or an upset VIP. Just be sure that the role play situation is relevant to the job.

Second, you must locate several people willing to be actors. The "actors" will take on, for example, the role of the angry customer or the press. Choose staff for actors who will be very good at "make believe" as they will need to make up the dialog and the emotions during the role play. Provide the actors with an orientation so that they will know what to do and how to interact. During the orientation, let the actors know what will be the personality of the character that they are playing. Do you want the actors to be stubborn? Angry no matter what? Demanding or arrogant? Remind people to stay in character throughout the role play as with amateur actors it is very easy to slip out of character. Actors out of character will damage the mood and the purpose of role-playing.

Depending upon the scale of the role-playing and the number of candidates being interviewed, you may want to consider having observers during each role play who can evaluate the candidate for you. The actors can also perform that function. Whether you are utilizing someone else's help or do the evaluation of the candidate, be sure to provide adequate training so that everyone knows what you want.

Third, the time must be set aside for role-playing. Most role-playing takes at least a half hour, many take an hour or more. This means that a lot of staff time will be invested in acting, observing, or evaluating role-playing.

Next, space must be set aside for role-playing. Obviously, the room must be private and spacious enough to accommodate everyone. Be sure to have all the "props" there too such as flip charts or whiteboards as needed.

Written instructions should also be given to the candidates. The instructions should include the time frame, a description of the organizational context and a description of the problem that the candidates have to resolve. Let the candidates know what their role is as well as the role of the actors. For example, Actor A will be a dissatisfied customer. Actor B will be the CEO. Actor C will be a major supplier. What you will not describe in the instructions is what direction the actors will take or what reactions they will have. That part must surprise the candidate.

Whether you want to give the instructions out to the candidates right before the process or several days before is the same issue as with making a presentation. The question is do you want to see how well the candidates think on their feet or how well they can prepare?

What are we looking for when evaluating role-playing? First of all, are the candidates using judgment and common sense? Do they show leadership ability? Is their decision-making sound? Are they concerned for people? Are they making the right decision for the organization? Are they assertive in difficult situations? Are they supportive of the policies and directions of the organization? Do they have understanding of a situation? Are they listening well? Are they participative and democratic in approach? If the answer to all of these questions is yes, you probably have a good candidate for the job.

Lastly, observe the candidates' attitudes towards the role play. Were they good at make-believe? Did they have a sarcastic or supercilious attitude towards it? Did they break out of character often? Look for the person who goes whole-heartedly into role-playing. In such a person, there will be both imagination and commitment.

POINT 4: CONDUCT AN IN-BASKET EXAM.

The in-basket exam is exactly what it sounds like. In this type of exam, a work day is simulated by having the candidates sit down at an in-basket and make decisions on the incoming items. Like role-playing, the in-basket exam also tests a candidate's ability to perform on the job. However, there is a lot less effort involved in setting up an in-basket exam than in setting up a role-playing exam.

To prepare for the in-basket exam, think once again about what skills are important for the job. Then, choose items that will test those skills. For example, if the job calls for someone who can set priorities, then the in-basket should contain items that have high but conflicting priorities. If the job calls for someone who has to do a lot of scheduling, then the in-basket should contain items in which there are a lot of scheduling problems.

Do give the candidate a fixed time in which to perform the test. This exam does test for speed of thought as well as for the ability to think appropriately. Moreover, every candidate has to have the same time frame so that no candidate is unfairly advantaged by having more time.

When reviewing the candidate's work on the in-basket exam, have in mind already what were the best solutions to the problems. Do be flexible on what is the right answer. A creative candidate might come up with an innovative idea. Consider discussing with the candidates their decisions on the paperwork. This will give you additional information as to why the candidates made certain decisions.

There are two drawbacks with the in-basket exam. First, there is the time involved for you and your staff. It does take a considerable amount of time to prepare the written documents for the in-basket. It also takes quite a bit of time to evaluate what the candidate has done. Make sure that the position calls for this extra investment of time.

Second, the in-basket exam tends to test how well people do paperwork even if that paperwork has human problems to solve. Therefore, if you really are interested in a candidate's people or social skills, it would be better to choose role-playing or spend more time at lunch with the candidate.

POINT 5: TAKE THE CANDIDATE ON A TOUR.

If you have a facility that is any size, consider taking the candidate on a tour of the building. There are two reasons for this. First, sometimes it is important in an interview that the candidate be seen by more than just the supervisor of the position. You may want the candidate to meet staff or other managers with whom the candidate might be interacting on the job. Taking the candidate on a tour enables all interested parties to see the candidate and to feel involved in the interview process. Ask people afterwards how they liked the candidate. Their opinion or insight might contain information for you later on when you are evaluating the candidate. Do remember though that their view of the candidate was very brief so do not let their opinions determine the fate of the candidate. Instead, use their opinions to supplement the interview process.

A tour also helps the candidate. A candidate needs as much information about people and place as possible in order to make a decision to accept the job if offered. It helps candidates to see all the personalities and to judge for themselves whether or not they will fit in. The candidates also will have an opportunity to see the physical place including the desk or office in which they might be working. People have a gut level reaction as to whether or not they like a place, so it is only fair to the candidates to let them see where they will be working.

It is good to keep the tour as informal as possible. Just walk the candidate around and introduce people as you catch them. This casual approach will allow for informal conversations from which both you and the candidate will learn things about each other. The only time you might want to schedule would be with any high level bosses who might not be available on short notice.

Remember to keep evaluating the candidate while you are touring. Some of the things that you should look for when the candidate goes on tour is the candidate's ability to interact with strangers, to have informal conversations, to answer questions, to ask intelligent questions, and to maintain an energy level with so much interaction.

One word of caution. Some candidates prefer for it not to be widely known that they are interviewing elsewhere and therefore would not be very happy with touring. You should respect this need. Touring can give you some good information about the candidate but it is not critical so the integrity of the interview will not be jeopardized if it does not occur.

POINT 6: GIVE THE CANDIDATE TIME ALONE.

Often these supplemental processes are held back to back with the interview. This means that the candidate will spend a considerable amount of time in the organization.

Whenever candidates will be spending a long time at the interview site, be sure to give them sometime to themselves. Interviewing, as we all know, is hectic and stressful. It is only courteous to let the candidates have time in the restroom alone, sit alone for awhile to draw their energy back in or to compose their thoughts. They will definitely appreciate this opportunity and will thank you for your thoughtfulness.

POINT 7: MANAGE THE TELEPHONE INTERVIEW

Sometimes because of the cost of flying or other inhibiting factors, the candidate is unable to come to the face-to-face interview. You may wish to extend the interview process by interviewing the candidate by phone.

First of all, make sure the logistics of the telephone interview are set up properly. You can either have a direct call between you, a conference call between the candidate, you and the other panelists, or have yourself and the panelists in a room with the candidate on the speaker phone. Personally, if you have panelists, I prefer the latter because it helps the interview go more smoothly when the interviewers, at least, can see each other.

Make sure that everyone involved with the interview is in a quiet place and will not be disturbed. I recommend that the candidate be at home rather than at work unless the person is very sure that he or she will not be disturbed. This interview should be conducted with the same privacy as the face-to-face interview.

Of course, have a previously scheduled time for the call just as you would any other interview. As a matter of courtesy, you should make the call rather than the candidate calling you. This way the candidate does not incur long distance charges.

Additional courtesy must be observed during the telephone interview if more than two people are involved. Since not everyone can see each other, it is harder to determine when one party has finished. Therefore, there are usually more pauses and more interruptions. Good humor will take everyone through this awkwardness.

The hardest thing about the telephone interview is that the all important factor of body language is missing. There is simply no substitute for seeing a person face to face. Therefore, since you have only the candidate's voice to go on and the logic of the candidate's answers, ask more questions than would ordinarily be asked of a candidate sitting next to you. Probe the candidate's background and education more. Ask the candidate to elaborate on the answers. The more that the candidate talks, the more information you will have.

In general, it is not wise to hire for any position when the candidate has never been seen in person. Too much information about the candidate is lost when the body language is invisible. The stakes are too high to hire a full-time permanent employee on the strength of voice alone. For this reason, I would recommend using the telephone interview as a preliminary screening process and then, if you like the person, have the face-to-face interview.

CONCLUSION

Since many of these supplemental processes are expensive, time-consuming or awkward, make sure that the situation really warrants the effort. The position should be important enough or special enough in some way to justify the additional work involved.

Supplemental processes should be as carefully crafted and administered as the oral interview itself. The supplemental processes should be seen as an important source of information about the candidate. Ultimately, this information should never take the place of the oral interview itself.

EXTENDING THE INTERVIEW PROCESS

QUICK CHECK

Point 1: Take the candidate to lunch.

- Have all of the logistics of the lunch been arranged?
- Has it been decided who will go on the lunch?
- Did everyone remember that the rules of interviewing still apply at lunch?
- Have you evaluated the candidate on their social skills?
- Were difficult restaurants avoided?
- Did the candidate handle alcohol well?

Point 2: Ask the candidate to make a speech.

- Will the speech be prepared or off the cuff?
- Were the candidates given a topic?
- Were the candidates given a time frame?
- Will the speech be videotaped?
- Was the speech interesting? Lively? Imaginative? Logical?

Point 3: Role play with the candidate.

- Is there enough staff to role-play?
- Is there enough time to role-play?

- Is role playing necessary?
- Were the candidates evaluated on judgment? Interaction? Assertiveness? Listening abilities? Decision-making?
- What was the candidate's attitude towards role-playing?

Point 4: Conduct an in-basket exam.

- Do you know what skills need to be identified?
- Has it been considered how the in-basket test should be graded?
- Were the candidates given a fixed time to take the test?
- Did you discuss the in-basket exam with the candidate?

Point 5: Take the candidate on a tour.

- Are there other people who need to meet the candidate?
- Have the visits with the boss or bosses been scheduled?
- Did you ask the staff their opinions about the candidate?
- Did the candidate need the interview to be relatively confidential?

Point 6: Give the candidate time alone.

- Have the candidates been allowed time by themselves to rest and relax?

Point 7: Manage the telephone interview.

- Have you arranged for a proper time and place for the interview?
- Do you have more questions to ask the candidate than usual?
- Have you probed the candidate's background to allow the candidate to talk more?
- Did you use the telephone interview as a screening process only?

6 CHOOSING THE CANDIDATE

POINTS TO REMEMBER

Point 1: Evaluate the personality of the candidate.
Point 2: Evaluate the experience and skills of the candidate.
Point 3: Evaluate the educational background.
Point 4: Gamble on inexperience with potential.
Point 5: Evaluate the answers.
Point 6: Consider the work group.
Point 7: Avoid early decisions.
Point 8: Don't compare the candidate with yourself.
Point 9: Don't focus on a single piece of information.
Point 10: Be aware of personal biases.
Point 11: Evaluate body language.
Point 12: Be aware of false notions.
Point 13: Don't falsely compare candidates.
Point 14: Do not discriminate against the pregnant candidate.
Point 15: Know why the candidate wants to change jobs.
Point 16: Watch for chronology.
Point 17: Examine the candidate's career.
Point 18: Determine how interested the candidate is.
Point 19: Remember no one is perfect.
Point 20: Don't let ego get in the way.
Point 21: Consider diversity in the workplace.
Point 22: Simulate the candidate in the workplace.
Point 23: Evaluate the candidate's questions.
Point 24: Review basic behavior.
Point 25: Don't feel sorry for the candidate.
Point 26: Remember skills develop but attitudes never change.
Point 27: Check references.
Point 28: Sleep overnight on the decision.
Point 29: Hire only when satisfied.
Point 30: Make the tough choices.
Point 31: Maintain records.

CHOOSING THE CANDIDATE

It is tempting to give into the feeling that the interview process is over once we walk the candidate to the door. However, even though the face-to-face interview is complete, the interview process is not complete until the candidates are evaluated, the top candidate selected, and the job offered and accepted. In this chapter, we will look at how to evaluate the candidates and select the best candidate for the job.

Evaluation of candidates calls for a lot of skill and effort if we want to end up with the best person. When we evaluate a candidate, we must utilize all of our judgment, intuition, and rationality. We have to accurately interpret the interview so that the brief window in time in which we saw the candidate becomes an accurate representation of the candidate's abilities. We have to check references where we must be able to ascertain the value of another person's opinion of the candidate. We have to have an understanding of character and an ability to match observable data with our own intuition. Is it any wonder that the wrong candidate is sometimes chosen?

Choosing the best candidate is challenging but very rewarding. By following the points in this chapter, you will be able to select the best candidate possible for the job.

POINT 1: EVALUATE THE PERSONALITY OF THE CANDIDATE.

As we have discussed before, the skills and abilities of the candidate alone are not enough. The candidate also must have the right personality for the job in order to be a good match for the position. Stop for a moment and think about the personality of the job and the personality of the candidate. Does the job require working with the public? If it does, then was the candidate personable and outgoing? Does the job require someone to sit all day doing detailed work? If it does, then was the candidate the type of person who can work quietly at a desk for eight hours? Does the job call for someone who is politically astute? If so, was the candidate diplomatic and tactful or blunt and plain-speaking? Clearly the latter characteristics, however refreshing, will soon create a lot of trouble in that job. In short, the personality of the candidate must fit the personality of the job. Remember that the right person must have the right personality to succeed.

Consider also how you like the personality of the candidate. Imagine yourself working with that person day after day, year after year. Was the candidate pleasant to be with? Was there a certain sparkle? As a final determiner, imagine how you would feel if the candidate was promoted over you one day and you had to work for that candidate. Do you still like the person now?

Having said all this, beware of snake charmers. There are a percentage of people who interview exceptionally well but whose performance on the job is poor. Their charm, personality, and winning attitudes carry them through every interview and make them very difficult to spot for what they really are. That is why we do not judge the candidate on a single factor alone but instead use many ways to assess the candidate's true worth.

However, the personality of the candidate is very important in determining job suitability so spend time thinking about and analyzing the candidate's personality traits.

POINT 2: EVALUATE THE EXPERIENCE AND SKILLS OF THE CANDIDATE.

Now, think about the experience and the skills of the candidate.

First, does the person have enough experience to perform well on the job? Remember that the candidate does not have to have all the experience necessary but enough to handle the job. Too much experience might lead to boredom and quite possibly moving on to another job. Too little, and the person will be in over his or her head.

Second, does the candidate's experience and skill point towards this job? Has there been a steady progression towards this type of position? Not that once in awhile a person can't make a real change but, in general, you want to look for someone for whom your vacant position is the next logical step. When people have moved steadily towards a certain type of position, they usually have the "seasoning" to handle the job.

Third, is there an adequate overlay of the candidate's skill set on the skill set required by the job? Does the candidate have, for example, the computer skills, the telephone skills, the public relations skills, or the supervisorial skills that you know will be needed for the job? Again, the candidate's skill set does not have to be a 100% overlay onto the job but still the minimum requirements should be met.

Fourth, has the candidate consistently shown growth? If a person has a life pattern of growth, the chances are considerable that this pattern will continue on this job. A person of growth is usually a more interesting, committed, and thoughtful employee. Showing growth is particularly important if you are looking for someone who will have the capability of eventually moving up in the job.

Fifth, does the candidate have other job experiences that could apply to this position? Don't be too narrow in reviewing the candidate's experiences. Besides the job history, look at a wide range of activities such as volunteer work, hobbies, and community activities. Some of these experiences give an indication of other capabilities of the candidate. Searching for additional or alternative experiences such as these is particularly important for young people who have little job history or for a mature personentering the job market for the first time or after many years of absence from work.

Lastly, did the candidate appear to learn from experience? Sometimes, it is as important to determine how well a candidate has learned from experience as to learn what those experiences were. Again, this indicates a person of growth and maturity.

FIGURE 6-1. Sample Desirable Characteristics for a Candidate

1. Helpful nature.
2. Well-trained for position.
3. Extroverted
4. Leadership potential
5. Strong service orientation
6. Friendly and welcoming.
7. Mature and realistic.
8. Receptive to change.
9. Independent and motivated.
10. Organization-minded.
11. Culturally aware.
12. Sound education or with breadth of knowledge.
13. Self-generating and initiating
14. Good communication skills.
15. Positive thinker
16. Good judgment
17. Creative and innovative.
18. Pleasant and courteous
19. Results-oriented

POINT 3: EVALUATE THE EDUCATIONAL BACKGROUND.

Although all of the candidates that you are evaluating have met the basic requirements for education, think now about any additional education that the candidate has that will be useful. Does the candidate speak a language other than English that could help with sales or international customers? Does the person have a knowledge of art or music or some other subject speciality that might be helpful in the job? Will the candidate be mixing with well-educated clients who will appreciate and expect a higher level of educational achievements? Does the candidate indicate any special certificates or licenses that could be useful?

While these additional educational elements will not help a candidate who does not have the experience and background for the job, it will help you when there are several finalists that you are considering. Such additional attainments in education can help a candidate move ahead of the pack.

POINT 4: GAMBLE ON INEXPERIENCE WITH POTENTIAL.

This point may seem to be a contradiction of the previous steps but if you spot real potential in a candidate you should seriously consider gambling on that candidate's ability. Most of the time we hire, for very good reasons, the more experienced person who demonstrates greater readiness for the job. However, once in awhile, the more experienced person may not be the best for the long run. Once in awhile, the less experienced individual, with a great deal of potential, will have much more capability for long-range success. Of course, you must judge which positon is appropriate for such a gamble to make sure that this person will not fail. It does little good to appoint even highly talented candidates to positions in which they will be completely in over their heads.

There are several benefits to hiring people with more potential than experience.

First of all, a candidate with potential is usually very grateful for obtaining what is clearly the chance of a lifetime. Such candidates are eager to demonstrate their ability so they usually perform with great energy and devotion to their work.

Secondly, a candidate who was given such a chance usually bonds to the supervisor that made that chance available. This means that you can develop a strong team. In turn, a strong team means that a lot of honesty, creativity, and productivity will prevail in the organization. In addition, depending upon the candidate's character, you may have a very supportive staff member which is one of the most pleasurable occurrences in a supervisor's life.

Lastly, your organization may become known as a fast track organization. A bright, young staff will be attracted to an organization that offers such possibilities for advancement and you may end up, over time, hiring many top candidates.

POINT 5: EVALUATE THE ANSWERS.

Recall now the interview itself and determine the general worth and value of the candidate's answers. Ask yourself these questions:

1. Was the candidate able to answer the questions in a way that showed mastery and understanding?
2. Were the answers thoughtful, well-rounded, to the point and balanced in judgment?
3. Did the candidate demonstrate that that the job had been thought about in depth before?
4. Did the answers show insight into and an understanding of the position?
5. Were the responses complete?
6. Did the candidate show an ability to look at many different aspects of a situation?
7. Did the candidate demonstrate the ability both to prepare and to follow through?
8. Did the candidate show maturity beyond their years?
9. Did the candidate demonstrate growth?
10. Is the candidate ambitious and hard-working?
11. Did the candidate show eagerness and enthusiasm for the job?
12. Was the candidate listening well?

An affirmative answer to these questions are a strong indication that you have a good candidate on your hands. Remember to look deeply and honestly at all the responses without being influenced by the charm or personality that the candidates exhibited.

POINT 6: CONSIDER THE WORK GROUP.

When evaluating the candidate, it is important to take into consideration the group with whom this candidate will work. Is the work group shy and quiet or vital and vivacious? Is it warm and friendly or cool and self-sufficient? Is there a task orientation with high performance standards or a people orientation with a relaxed attitude? It is important to understand the personality of the work group in order to select a candidate who will "fit in" and get along with the rest of the group.

If the new person does not fit in with the group, there can be several consequences. A major area of concern is that disparate personalities never develop the teamwork so necessary to a successful unit. Too many differences in personality and style block good communication and can cause employee conflict. One test is to ask yourself—if the work group and the new employee were at a party, would they seek each other out for the enjoyment of each other's company? If yes, you may have a match. If no, you may have a problem.

Another area of concern is the loneliness of the new employee that does not fit in. People who are lonely at work are often easily alienated. Worse, a lonely person with a less mature character, may team up with a problem employee. Problem employees always need a supporter and will go instinctively towards a person who has nowhere else to go. Then, you might have two problem employees.

Now, this does not mean that we hire clones so that everyone in a work group is a replica of the other. Only that it appears, from your best judgment, that the person will get along with the others.

You might be saying to yourself about now, "I am not looking for my employees to have a relationship, just to get the work done". This is true but none of us can afford to be naieve about the consequences of incompatible workers. Incompatibility is one of the root causes of employee conflict which is a major problem for most supervisors.

When we take the work group into consideration, we have to realize that the best person in an interview pool is not the same as the best person for the job. Each job has a unique set of circumstances and you, the interviewer, need to be sensitive to the issues of candidate compatibility by looking at the total job not just the skill set and salary match of the candidate.

One last thought: What if you are not happy with the work group and want a whole different personality there? In that case, you need to consider putting in someone with a different personality as the first of a new wave of change. Of course, make sure that the candidate is strong and independent of nature as this is a little hard on the new person who may struggle with loneliness and alienation and the hostility of fellow employees.

POINT 7: AVOID EARLY DECISIONS.

It is very easy in an interview process to decide too early which candidate gets the job. Sometimes we are influenced by outside pressures, long lines at service desks as a result of inadequate staffing, backlogs or high vacancy rates to hurry and commit to a candidate. If you can, resist all of these pressures and avoid making early decisions on a candidate until you have had time to evaluate the candidates fully. If you hurry and miss some portion of evaluating, you run the risk of hiring the wrong candidate. The consequences of hiring the wrong person must always be considered before you dash off to make a decision. Anyone who hurries to hire a new employee because of time pressures should remember about all the time that will be needed to remove the wrong person from the position.

POINT 8: DON'T COMPARE THE CANDIDATE WITH YOURSELF.

Don't compare the candidate with yourself. Using yourself as a standard for hiring is not at all the same as using an objective set of standards for the job. Just because you have certain values or personality traits does not mean that they are the desired characteristics for the job.

Moreover, remember to consider the importance of diversity in the workplace. Diversity makes for a multi-talented organization. Try not to develop a work group filled with people that are clones of yourself.

Actually, the only time that you should consider your own personality as a major consideration is when you are hiring a personal secretary, an assistant, or someone with whom you will work very closely. In these cases, we all need someone who blends very well with our personalities.

POINT 9: DON'T FOCUS ON A SINGLE PIECE OF INFORMATION.

Sometimes, in the process of evaluating a candidate, we cannot get out of our heads something that the candidate has said. Usually, this "something" is negative and it has power to influence us in our decisions about a candidate. Now, of course, we should have clarified this comment while the interview was underway. However, if this was not done, the "something" can remain to haunt us.

Unless the comment was singularly glaring or devastating, try not to focus on this single piece of data about the candidate. Sometimes people, out of anxiety, do mis-speak, even though they might be a perfectly good candidate. Instead, focus on the entire range of responses from the candidate. Be sure to look at the larger picture of the candidate's life and career and not get carried away overreacting to a single comment.

If you really like the candidate and want to give him or her serious consideration but that one piece of information troubles you, you may need to have a second interview or perhaps even take the candidate to lunch. It is better to take the extra time needed to speak with the candidate again than lose a potentially good candidate. However, only contact the candidate again when you are very serious about this candidate as a possible hire.

Of course, during this second interview or lunch, you will have to include your question amidst other areas of discussion so that it is not obvious to the candidate that you are fishing for one piece of information. Having just a single focus will puzzle or trouble the candidate. Also, be careful not to give any indication of a job promise because of a second interview.

POINT 10: BE AWARE OF PERSONAL BIASES.

We have already spoken about the need to protect candidates from our biases when we were conducting the interview. Remind yourself again to watch out for your personal biases when you are evaluating the candidates.

A bias is prejudice against a certain characteristic, style, culture, or approach to life. Biases are irrational. Most were programmed in us in childhood when we were unable to reason properly. As adults, we carry these biases deep in our brains.

Be aware of your personal biases. Just because you don't like candidates who are too heavy or too thin or too tall or too short or the opposite sex or another race, doesn't mean that you have to act on it. No superficial characteristics such as body type or color should influence your decision about a candidate. Look beyond the superficial characteristics to the person inside. Your only decision should be whether or not the candidate is the best person for the job.

POINT 11: EVALUATE BODY LANGUAGE.

Effective communication skills are essential for success on any job. However, as we all know, communication is based on so much more than words. In fact, studies have demonstrated that 90% of all communication is through body language. Therefore, if you want someone who will communicate effectively on the job, you must choose someone who has good body language.

Ask yourself about the body language of the candidate. Were the gestures appropriate? Did the candidate's movements put everyone at ease? Did the candidate smile and laugh at the right times? Were the candidate's movements flowing and natural? Did the candidate reveal self-confidence but not cockiness? Did all the motions reveal an open character? Think about the body language of the candidates carefully because people out of sync with their own body will probably have difficulty communicating.

When evaluating body language, take into account that the person might have a different culture than your own. Different cultures mean different body languages. For example, people who grew up in the United States in the Anglo-Saxon tradition, deem it important to always look directly at the speaker. People who don't look at the speaker are thought to be sneaky or deceitful. In other cultures, looking away from the speaker might be a sign of respect. Be sensitive to other cultures and do not make assumptions about body language based upon your own behavior.

Also take in account the body language that comes from nervousness. The inappropriate laugh, the trembling, the fixed smile— all of these are rooted in nervousness and all of them should go away within a few minutes unless the interview is with an unusually terrified candidate. Now, if the nervousness did not go away in the interview, then you do need to consider if the level of nervousness was acceptable for the level of the position. For example, a candidate who is interviewing for an entry level position should be allowed to show more nervousness than a candidate interviewing for a higher level position. People at the higher levels are expected to and need to have more self-confidence in order to do the job.

Lastly, remember that persons with disabilities may have a body language that is different from your own. Their physical beings have certain limits that may inhibit the smooth movements that we have come to assume means good body language and communication. Just be aware of the differences so that you can assess the body language at a conscious level rather than reacting subconsciously, meaning negatively, to a movement or gesture that is different to you.

POINT 12: BE AWARE OF FALSE NOTIONS.

We all must be careful not to let false notions influence our evaluation of a candidate. False notions are formed when we make an irrational connection between superficial appearances or actions and the candidate's true behavior. For example, a candidate who is neat is not automatically efficient. A candidate who has a weak handshake is not necessarily weak. A candidate who is older is not necessarily mature. Such false notions get in the way of a true evaluation of the candidates' abilities.

Remember to judge the candidate on his or her total ability not on isolated characteristics. Try to get a complete picture of the candidate not a narrow one.

POINT 13: DON'T FALSELY COMPARE CANDIDATES.

The comparison of candidates is a natural part of the selection process. However, in the discussion of each candidate's skills and abilities, be careful not to falsely compare candidates as a result of this very common situation. It may happen that you interview a candidate who, in spite of the excellence of the person's resume and application, is absolutely awful in person. Once you have seen a bad candidate, the next candidate in the door usually looks much better than that candidate might have otherwise.

This situation also happens in reverse. Sometimes when we conclude an interview with a candidate with a really sparkling personality, the next one after the sparkler can look much worse than in reality.

Always make sure when you are evaluating candidates that you evaluate them either against an objective set of standards for the job or against another candidate's true skills and abilities. A candidate's accidental placement in the interview sequence should not affect your evaluation.

POINT 14: DO NOT DISCRIMINATE AGAINST THE PREGNANT CANDIDATE.

Everyone knows that it is against the law to discriminate against a pregnant candidate. However, when we see a pregnant candidate, often the first thought in our minds is that she will soon require an extended leave of absence, have child care problems, and need additional sick leave. A lot of good candidates are passed over because they are pregnant.

Remember that a candidate cannot be rejected because she is pregnant unless the pregnancy will prevent her from doing the job duties. For example, the job may require heavy lifting which she may not be able to do. However, if she is rejected, it must be because she cannot do heavy lifting not because she is pregnant. Additionally, remember that the burden is always on the employer to show that she cannot do the job.

Be flexible when the candidate is pregnant. Pregnancy is no reason to pass up a good candidate.

POINT 15: KNOW WHY THE CANDIDATE WANTS TO CHANGE JOBS.

Hopefully, during the interview you were able to ascertain why the candidate wants to change jobs. In order to evaluate the response, begin by considering now what the candidate's response was and matching that response to what is occuring in your workplace. For example, it does little good to hire any candidate who claims boredom in the current job when your job is very similar. It will not be long before the candidate is bored with your job too. Equally, it will do little good to hire a person who says there is no advancement in his or her current job when you know that your job has little chance for advancement either. It will not be long before this candidate is a candidate elsewhere.

Be especially careful when a candidate has said it was necessary to leave because of workplace problems such as a bad boss or employee conflicts. Try to ascertain from the response if the candidate was a contributing factor to the problems. Obviously, you do not want to hire someone else's problems. Particularly watch out for anyone who has a pattern of leaving because of problems.

POINT 16: WATCH FOR CHRONOLOGY.

You should have been able to ascertain during the interview whether or not there was any unusual job or education chronology of the candidate. Think for a moment now whether or not you were satisfied with the candidate's responses. Did the candidate explain satisfactorily why he or she had three jobs in three years? Could the candidate explain why he or she has only been on their current job for six months? Did you understand why the candidate took eight years to get through college? Were you satisfied as to why there was a four year gap in the candidate's career? All of these situations can have legitimate reasons. You must be convinced in your mind that the reasons were legitimate. Otherwise, you run the risk of hiring a job hopper, someone with an inability to focus or commit. In short, you might hire a problem employee.

POINT 17: EXAMINE THE CANDIDATE'S CAREER.

Think now about the path of the candidate's career. If the candidate's career appears to be plateauing or going downwards, seek a satisfactory explanation as to why? If the candidate's salary has taken a decline or has stayed the same for awhile, were you comfortable with the reasons? If the candidate is not working currently, did you feel that the candidate's reason for unemployment is a good one? Again, there may be many legitimate reasons for all of these incidences, some beyond the candidate's ability to control, but you must be satisfied that all these explanations are good ones. Otherwise, again you could run the risk of hiring a problem employee.

POINT 18: DETERMINE HOW INTERESTED THE CANDIDATE IS.

Studies have shown that about 80% of all people are in the wrong jobs. Is it any wonder that there are so many problems with employee morale and motivation? It is very important that a candidate be interested in the job for the content of the job itself. A candidate must have a lot of liking for the nature of the work in order to maintain a good level of motivation and morale. Candidates who are just trying to get out of a problem situation, who just want to move to a new location or who just want to get any promotion are not as interested in the nature of the job itself. These types of candidates, unless they have a great deal of self-discipline, have a higher probability of losing their motivation or having poor morale when they feel themselves locked into a job that does not suit them well.

Look closely at the level of interest that the candidate has in the position. Has the candidate shown a lot of commitment to this line of work? If so, there is the likelihood that the candidate likes the job for itself. If the candidate is switching careers or starting out new, were you satisfied through the interview that the candidate has enough motivation towards this line of work? Did the candidate ever attend seminars in the field, have hobbies that relate, do volunteer work, or take classes in the field? All of these activities may indicate an interest.

Try also to pick up on the subtle cueing that goes on during the interview. With close observation of the candidate, you should be able to pick up on the level of interest in the job. There is a certain drive, sparkle, and alertness that comes with a candidate who really wants a certain position. The candidate's preparation for the job is one obvious cue. A candidate who has gone to the work site, done background reading, and really thought about the position is bound to have more motivation.

POINT 19: REMEMBER THAT NO ONE IS PERFECT.

Once in awhile, you will find a candidate who is a perfect fit for the job. You will like everything there is about that candidate and will have that "go ahead" feeling. However, most people are not 100%. More often than not, there will always be some minor aspects about the candidate with which you are not completely happy. It might be that the candidate's experience is a little less than desired or the candidate may have slightly less ability to do some small aspect of the job. Minor weaknesses should not discourage you from an otherwise good candidate. Instead, ascertain if the candidate has the ability to develop these lesser skills. Of course, all of these weaknesses must be very minor otherwise you should not consider hiring the candidate.

POINT 20: DON'T LET EGO GET IN THE WAY.

Never let your ego get in the way of evaluating the candidate properly. The comment "I can size a person up within five seconds of meeting them" has no place in the modern interview. It is true that we can learn some things very quickly about people but it is also true that it takes years for a person's character to unfold. If we are stuck on our own ego and our own mistaken ability to size people up within seconds, then we cannot evaluate the candidate properly. All of us have to look at the facts of the interview, as well as our feelings, in order to make a proper evaluation. Your ability to judge character in a split second is not at question here. Don't let your ego get in the way of a real evaluation of a candidate's abilities.

POINT 21: CONSIDER DIVERSITY IN THE WORKPLACE.

Diversity in the workplace greatly enriches and enhances the organization's capabilities. People with different points of view, different frames of reference, different talents and backgrounds help to keep your workplace vital and thriving.

An organization filled with people who are too similar tend to view the world in limited directions. That degree of limitation is too dangerous in a world of so much change—no organization can survive for long, or survive well, with those kind of blinders.

It isn't always easy for us to hire people who are different from ourselves. It is only natural to feel more comfortable with people who are like us. However, our comfort levels are not the issue here. The issue is getting the right candidate who will make a real contribution to our workplace.

So, hire the opposite sex, people of different races and cultures, persons with disabilities, people whose native language is different from your own. Your workplace will be a lot more vital, interesting and responsive as a result.

POINT 22: SIMULATE THE CANDIDATE IN THE WORKPLACE.

Sometimes it helps to simulate in our minds what the candidate would be like on the job. Sit back for a moment and imagine the candidate coming to work, interacting with fellow employees, joining in on meetings, dealing with customers, speaking on the phone, solving problems, talking with you. These simulations help to bring the candidate into perspective in the actual environment and also help to bring a level of reality of what it would be like to really hire that candidate. If you cannot see the candidate fitting in in your mind, then chances are the candidate won't fit in in reality.

POINT 23: EVALUATE THE CANDIDATE'S QUESTIONS.

Sometimes what candidates ask of us can be as interesting as the answers that they give to the interview questions. Think now about what the candidate asked and evaluate those questions. Did the questions reveal the candidate's priorities for the job? Were the questions honest and straight-forward? Were the concerns of the candidate appropriate to the level of the job? Was the candidate aggressive or defensive with the questions? Was the candidate too concerned with benefits? Was the candidate more interested in what the organization was going to do for him or her than in what the candidate was going to do for the organization? Was the candidate more interested in job security than opportunity? Look closely at the questions and analyze what was asked and how it was asked. The questions will tell you what was on the mind of a candidate. You must judge whether what was on the candidate's mind matches what you need on the job.

POINT 24: REVIEW BASIC BEHAVIOR.

Don't forget to evaluate these four very basic but important elements of the candidate's behavior.

1. Was the candidate consistently polite to secretarial or other staff when you were not there to see or hear? A person who only has manners for people with power reveals an unpleasant character. Ask the staff about the candidate.
2. Was the candidate on time for the interview? Sometimes accidents can occur that create lateness but a candidate on time shows eagerness, good manners, respect, and organization.
3. Did the candidate have a smile and a friendly manner? Warmth goes a long way. It is difficult to work with people all day long who are cold or unfriendly.
4. Was the candidate attentive to appearance? A person who is neat and appropriately dressed reveals respect for the job. Be careful though in judging young people too harshly on dress because they often just do not have the job experience to know what to wear and may not have anyone at home to advise them.

Just make a note of the candidate's behavior in these areas and add them to your overall evaluation of the candidate.

POINT 25: DON'T FEEL SORRY FOR THE CANDIDATE.

Sometimes when we are interviewing candidates we feel sorry for them and give them a higher rating than they might deserve. There are many reasons why our compassion and interest can be triggered. Sometimes the candidate reminds us of a much younger version of ourselves. Sometimes we can see that the candidate is desperate for any job. Sometimes we just like the candidate a lot even if the skills, experience, and education required is just not there. Sometimes the candidate is just trying so hard.

You must be alert to your feelings but must not act upon them regardless of the reason. Remember that you are looking for the best candidate for the position. Your compassion and interest in the candidate, however worthy, should not cloud a true evaluation of the candidate's worth.

POINT 26: REMEMBER SKILLS DEVELOP BUT ATTITUDES NEVER CHANGE.

It is natural for us to want to hire a person who is highly skilled for the job. Sometimes, though, we are tempted to hire a person who has excellent technical knowledge for the job but who lacks a good attitude. Don't let any skill take precedence over the person's attitude. People can increase their skills tremendously on the job. However, attitudes rarely change. If you hire a person who is negative, complaining, or sour, the probability of that person changing attitudes is very low. Rarely does a person develop the self-awareness later in life to change. Moreover, even if the bad attitude can be changed, it usually is at great cost to you. Why would you want to invest that kind of time or effort into a new employee? Hire people who have a positive, constructive manner who will make a real contribution to the workplace.

POINT 27: CHECK REFERENCES.

One of the most vital components of a candidate's evaluation is the checking of references. Let me say this plainly. You should not hire any candidate without making every effort to check references. Remember that, when all is said and done, an interview is only a relatively small period of time in which to test a candidate's abilities. Reference checking expands that period of time by letting you see what the candidate's performance is like day to day on the job.

First of all, make sure that the candidate has at least three references. Three references will give you a more balanced view of the candidate. Do ask what the relationship of the references are to the candidate. It does little good to have references from close colleagues and family friends. Inevitably, they will recommend the candidate for the job. It is much better to speak with people who have supervised the candidate. Other supervisors know the cost of hiring a problem employee and, unless they are unethical, restricted by company policy or want to dump the candidate at any price, they will tell you at least something about the candidate's performance.

Include in the reference check the candidate's most recent supervisor. This is the best person to tell about the candidate's current abilities. Now, sometimes checking with the candidate's boss is a problem for the candidate. Not all bosses are liberal about their staff looking for other jobs. Be respectful of the candidate's concern but insistent as to its importance. Sooner or later, you have to speak with the current supervisor of the candidate. More often than not, when a candidate does not want a potential employer to speak with the boss, the candidate is having a problem with the boss. You need to know that. However, in consideration for those candidates who just have tough bosses who really will be upset if they are leaving, arrange with these candidates to call their bosses right before the job offer if it occurs. All of the other references can be called first.

You may want to consider getting written permission from all the candidates to call their references. Have the candidates sign a waiver form that authorizes you to find out information about the candidate. This serves as some protection for you and for the person who will be giving you information about the candidate. Sometimes you will need to send the waiver form to the references so that they have a copy in their files in the event of any problems.

Sometimes the candidate will be carrying written references. Do read these references but still check on the candidate independently.

It is better to make phone calls than to do reference checking through the mail. For one thing, phone calls are faster. For another, people will tell a person information confidentially that they would never care to put in writing. Sometimes, you will encounter a company that only responds through the mail. Take what references can be obtained but be persistent without being a pest about trying to reach someone in person.

Do organize yourself before checking references. Know who the person is that you are calling and what that person's relationship is to the candidate. Have ready the list of questions to ask the person about the candidate. Be prepared to take copious notes. It is always surprising how much information can be forgotten from a conversation. You will need your notes to help you with your evaluation of the candidate and also to share with the panel if you have one.

Begin by identifying yourself and asking for what you want. Find out if this is a convenient time for the person to speak with you. Briefly explain about your organization and about the job. Do confirm basic information about the candidate such as current salary, employment dates and job duties. It is estimated that 10% of all people lie about their employment history.

Try to ask all of the questions that you have listed. Sometimes it is easy to get deflected away from the questions in the stream of conversation. Of course, no one should be so rigid about the questions that an interesting comment from the candidate's reference is passed over in the pursuit to finish the prepared questions.

If the candidate's reference does start to dodge questions or to avoid anything negative, don't be aggressive but do keep inquiring. Read between the lines. Ask penetrating and meaningful questions. Ask the same question in a couple of different ways if the issue is important. While the need to remain professionally courteous is essential, no person checking references should be drawn into a simple conversation. There is a lot at stake if the wrong person is hired. Remember to always close by asking all references if they would rehire this candidate. A simple yes or no to that question is very revealing.

Sometimes you may run into a person who cannot get references. The candidate may not have worked for a long time and anyone who could have given the candidate a reference has long since left. More often the case, the company for which the candidate is working has a policy of not giving references other than confirming that the candidate works there. Once again, try to get whatever references might be available. Do realize that there will be times when you will encounter candidates who cannot get references. When this happens, you must decide if there is enough information about the person through the interview to take a chance. While it is not recommended that a person be hired without references, occasionally we do want to take that risk if everything else looks really good.

Please be aware that sometimes real problem employees do try to cover up their past by not being able to give references. Make sure that the candidate really does not have references and is not just covering up a problem past.

Be prepared to use your professional networks in addition to the references provided. Call people who may know the candidate or who may know someone who does know the candidate. These pieces of information are very useful. Don't be afraid of gossip that is on the network but remember that it is just gossip. However, if you do hear anything negative about the candidate, it would be worthwhile to check it out.

Consider checking the references of the top three candidates as opposed to only checking the references of the top candidate. Sometimes a person might do a lesser interview but have sparkling references. References can change your mind about a candidate.

SAMPLE REFERENCE CHECK QUESTIONS

1. In what capacity did you know the applicant and for how long?
2. What specifically was his/her work assignment?
3. How would you rate his/her:
   a. performance
   b. supervisory abilities
   c. ability to get along with others
   d. work habits
   e. creativity
   f. leadership abilities
   g. ability to work independently
4. What were the circumstances regarding his/her leaving?
5. Would you rehire him/her?
6. What are his/her strengths?
7. What are his/her weaknesses?
8. Would you consider him/her suitable for the position I am filling?
9. Did he/she follow through on assignments?
10. Did he/she comply with instructions/directions?
11. Did he/she have a positive attitude?
12. Is he/she a self-starter?
13. Does he/she have good judgment?
14. Does he/she have a good relationship with the boss?
15. Is he/she good with customers?
16. Is he/she able to solve problems?
17. Is he/she a part of the team?
18. What will be the reaction at work if he/she announces his/her resignation?
19. Is there anything else that you could tell me about this candidate?

POINT 28: SLEEP OVERNIGHT ON THE DECISION.

Never be eager in hiring. Always take a day and a night to let the hiring decision germinate in your mind. The mind needs to rest from the information overload of interviewing and reference checking. Thinking overnight can sometimes shed new light on the candidates. It is surprising what clarity can come in the morning even if there was confusion the night before.

You should make it a habit to sleep overnight on the hiring decision even if you are sure that you have the right candidate. When the subconscious has time to process information overnight, sometimes a formerly clear decision might look a little different. Give yourself this extra time to make sure that you are choosing the right candidate.

POINT 29: HIRE ONLY WHEN SATISFIED.

When a job vacancy occurs, we often feel a sense of urgency to fill the position so that we can move forward with the work. There is no doubt that one of the most difficult decisions to make is not to fill a position when we do not feel that any of the candidates are suitable for the job. Remember the mission is not to fill the position with any candidate but to fill the position with the right candidate.

Sometimes we will be under pressure from the staff to fill the position as soon as possible. After all, they are picking up the extra workload, dealing with customer pressures, long lines, backlogs, or unmet schedules. Just remind them that it is still easier to have these problems than to have the wrong, and potentially a problem, employee in the job. Hiring the wrong person helps no one.

If you find yourself in this situation, just start the search again. Better a vacancy than a problem employee. You must be sure that you have the right candidate before offering the job.

POINT 30: MAKE THE TOUGH CHOICES.

Once in awhile, it will occur that you have not one but two excellent candidates for a single job. Both candidates may have interviewed well. Both may have great personalities and both might have terrific references. Among the many predicaments that you can be in, the predicament of choosing between two top candidates is not a bad one. The difficulty is that you may be very torn, sometimes for days at a time, trying to decide between the two candidates. There are really only three ways that you can solve this predicament.

First, consider who will be the best candidate in the long run. A lot of candidates look good for the job now but you must ask what will be the long term contribution of this candidate? What is this person's potential? Choose the candidate who, in the long-run, will make the most contribution.

Second, simulate. Simulate in your mind what it is like offering the job to one candidate and turning down the other. If you feel a greater sense of loss with one candidate than the other, you probably have a preference for that candidate.

Lastly, you may want to call the candidates in for a second interview. If you spend enough time with a candidate, sooner or later a preference for one or the other will emerge.

Once the top candidate is chosen, be prepared for experiencing a feeling of regret that both candidates could not be hired. It is very difficult to let a good candidate get away. Do keep the candidate who was turned down in mind for future positions.

POINT 31: MAINTAIN RECORDS.

Be sure to maintain records of the evaluation for a few months. Document your decision, the comments of other panelists and the results of your reference checking. Occasionally, there are problems with hiring and it is better if you work from written documentation rather than memory.

CONCLUSION

Choosing the candidate is the most important decision that you will make in the interview process. Be thorough, thoughtful, and insightful. You will have to live with the consequences of your decision for a very long time.

CHOOSING THE CANDIDATE

QUICK CHECK

Point 1: Evaluate the personality of the candidate.

- Does the personality of the job match the personality of the candidate?
- Do you like this person?
- Is the person a snake charmer?

Point 2: Evaluate the experience and skills of the candidate.

- Does the person have enough experience to perform well on the job?
- Does the candidate's background point towards this job?
- Has the candidate consistently shown growth?
- Are there other job experiences that might apply?
- Has the candidate learned from experience?

Point 3: Evaluate the educational background.

- Does the person have some specialized knowledge?
- Does the candidate have another language?
- Does the candidate have any special certificates?

Point 4: Gamble on inexperience with potential.

- Do you have a candidate with a lot of potential?
- Will this be a good person for the long run?
- Will the person be in over his or her head?

Point 5: Evaluate the answers.

- Did the candidate show job knowledge?
- Did the candidate show maturity and judgment?
- Did the candidate show job preparation?
- Were the answers well-thought out?
- Were the responses complete?

Point 6: Consider the work group.

- Will the candidate fit in with the group?
- Will you be able to develop a team?

Point 7: Avoid early decisions.

- Are you under pressure to make too fast a decision?
- Was any portion of the evaluation process missed?
- Have the consequences of hiring the wrong person been considered?

Point 8: Don't compare the candidate with yourself.

- Are you using yourself as a standard of hiring?
- Is there diversity in the workplace?

Point 9: Don't focus on a single piece of information.

- Has a small piece of negative data influenced you?
- Have you verified or clarified this information?
- Are you focusing on the larger picture of the candidate?

Point 10: Be aware of personal biases.

- Do you have any biases?
- Are you conscious of personal biases when candidates are being rated?

Point 11: Evaluate body language.

- Does the person have good body language?
- Were other cultural backgrounds taken into account?
- Is the candidate just nervous?

Point 12 Be aware of false notions.

- Has a false connection between appearances and behavior been made?
- Are candidates being judged on their total ability?

Point 13: Don't falsely compare candidates.

- Has a disappointing candidate made everyone else look good?
- Has a sparkling candidate made everyone else look bad?

Point 14: Do not discriminate against the pregnant candidate.

- Has a candidate been rejected just because she is pregnant?
- Are you aware of the law that pertains to pregnant candidates?

Point 15: Know why the candidate wants to change jobs.

- Do you know the reasons why a candidate wants to change jobs?
- Is the candidate having any problems in the workplace?
- Is the candidate covering up a reason for leaving?

Point 16: Watch for chronology.

- Has the chronology of a person's career been evaluated?
- Are there any absences that are unexplained in work history?
- Has the person taken too long to go through school?

Point 17: Examine the candidate's career.

- Is the candidate going up or down in his or her career?
- Has the candidate plateaued in his or her career?
- Has the candidate been laid off from a higher job?
- Does the direction of the candidate's career suit this job?

Point 18: Determine how interested a candidate is.

- Do you know what the candidate's motivation is for taking this job?
- Has the candidate demonstrated adequate preparation and motivation?

Point 19: Remember that no one is perfect.

- Were minor weaknesses overlooked?
- Does it seem if the person will grow on the job?

Point 20: Don't let ego get in the way.

- Did you let your ego get in the way of the evaluation?
- Are you using more than just feelings to evaluate the candidate?

Point 21: Consider diversity in the workplace.

- Do you value diversity in the workplace?
- Is your own comfort level influencing your decision?

Point 22: Simulate the candidate in the workplace.

- Have you simulated the presence of the candidate in the workplace?

Point 23: Evaluate the candidate's questions.

- Did you analyze the candidate's questions?
- Was the candidate's concerns appropriate?
- Did the candidate demonstrate a good sense of priorities?

Point 24: Review basic behavior.

- Was the candidate on time?
- Was the candidate neat and appropriately dressed?
- Was the candidate polite to everyone?
- Was the candidate warm and friendly?

Point 25: Don't feel sorry for the candidate.

- Do you feel compassion for the candidate?
- Is your compassion clouding your judgment?
- Is your evaluation of the candidate being influenced?

Point 26: Remember skills develop but attitudes never change.

- Have you allowed the person's technical skills to completely influence your decision?

- Does the person have a good attitude?
- Do you want to spend the time to change a negative employee?

Point 27: Check references.

- Did you call the candidate's supervisor?
- Do you have a prepared list of questions?
- Are you checking by phone rather than by mail?
- Are you taking notes when speaking to the references?
- Was the professional network used?
- Do you want to check the references of all the top candidates?

Point 28: Sleep overnight on the decision.

- Are you too eager to hire?
- Did you give the decision time for mature deliberation?

Point 29: Hire only when satisfied.

- Are you only moving forward only when feeling great about a candidate?
- Are you just trying to fill a vacancy?

Point 30: Make the tough choices.

- Are there two top candidates?
- Have you considered who is the best in the long run?
- Is a second interview needed?
- Will the other candidate be kept in mind for a future job?

Point 31: Maintain records.

- Did you document your decision?
- Have you saved the records?

FIGURE 6-1. Sample Desirable Characteristics for a Candidate

1. Helpful nature.
2. Well-trained for position.
3. Extroverted
4. Leadership potential
5. Strong service orientation
6. Friendly and welcoming.
7. Mature and realistic.
8. Receptive to change.
9. Independent and motivated.
10. Organization-minded.
11. Culturally aware.
12. Sound education or with breadth of knowledge.
13. Self-generating and initiating
14. Good communication skills.
15. Positive thinker
16. Good judgment
17. Creative and innovative.
18. Pleasant and courteous
19. Results-oriented

7 OFFERING THE JOB

POINTS TO REMEMBER

Point 1: Prepare the offer.
Point 2: Negotiate salary effectively.
Point 3: Approach the candidate properly.
Point 4: Compete effectively with other offers.
Point 5: Accepting no for an answer.
Point 6: Negotiate the start date.
Point 7: Give time for consideration.
Point 8: Make special arrangements.
Point 9: Demonstrate courtesy.
Point 10: Confirm in writing.

OFFERING THE JOB

Obviously, the interview process is not complete until the chosen candidate has accepted the job offer. Surprisingly enough, it is not uncommon for a candidate to go all the way through the interview process only to turn down the job at the last moment. There are many reasons for this. First of all, when people are confronted with the actual reality of making a job change, they re-evaluate who they are and what they want in life. That process of discovery can sometimes go against an organization making a genuine job offer. Next, circumstances, such as a sudden illness in the family, can alter the candidate's decision to change positions at that time. Third, sometimes a candidate will participate wholeheartedly all the way through the interview process only to decide that he or she really does not like the organization, does not care for the job or the person for whom they will be working. This third point is a good reminder to all of us to remember that as we are observing the candidate so also is the candidate observing us. Lastly, sometimes candidates turn down the job because of the way that the job offer has been managed.

The first three reasons for turning down the job are usually beyond our control. What is within our control is the way the job was offered and the negotiations conducted. Organizations reveal themselves in every action that they take just as people do. A job offer that is badly managed can turn off a candidate from working there. A positive experience in the job offer can encourage a candidate to accept the position. Therefore, we have to learn how to make a good job offer to get the response that we want and to start the candidate off on the right foot with our organization.

Let's look now at the best ways to offer the job.

POINT 1: PREPARE THE OFFER.

Before calling the candidate to offer the job, be sure to prepare in advance what you will say to the candidate. The conversation between you and the candidate is very important. Everything needs to be together in your mind so that the job can be discussed seriously with the candidate. Think through what you are going to say and anticipate what the candidate may ask. At the very least, you should be prepared to discuss the salary, the benefits, start date, and any questions about the nature of the job that might still be unclear in the candidate's mind.

Treat the job offer with real respect. The step of leaving a job is a very big one for any candidate and it must be handled with sensitivity and understanding. The candidate will appreciate your professionalism.

As a footnote, make sure that you have consulted with your boss if necessary before you make the job offer. Some bosses give completely free rein, others like to be informed ahead of time.

POINT 2: NEGOTIATE SALARY EFFECTIVELY.

Negotiating a salary is much like any kind of bargaining. You will make what you think is a reasonable offer to the candidate. The candidate will return with a higher counter offer—usually higher than the candidate expects to get in the end. You make another offer and with some discussion and understanding on both sides, an agreement is reached. It sounds easy, doesn't it? Let's look more closely.

Before offering the job, be clear in your mind exactly what the salary offer is that you will make. You should also be clear about how far you are willing to negotiate. In other words, what is the top price that you are is willing to pay for this candidate? Are you willing to lose the candidate if the candidate's salary demands cannot be met? Of course, sometimes there are budgetary limitations that prohibit meeting the candidate's demands. However, if budget is not a major issue and you are willing to lose the candidate rather than paying a higher salary then ask yourself how much you really want this candidate. Naturally, we are speaking about reasonable salary demands.

If a candidate makes an unreasonable demand and sticks to it without any budging, draw one of these four conclusions. First, the candidate's judgment is off about the organization or about their personal worth. You may want to reconsider your hiring decision on this candidate. You can let this candidate go by saying "I am sorry. We just cannot make your salary request. We appreciate your interest in us."

Second, the candidate might be making unreasonable demands so that he or she can back out of the offer. In this case, the candidate really does not want to change jobs and just wants to find an excuse to say no. This is particularly common with personality types who succumb to a lot of pressure on what they "should" be doing. Such candidates may actually like and enjoy their current positon but feel under some pressure that they "should" be advancing or "should" be making more money or "should" have a better way of life. Their dilemma as they struggle between their "shoulds" and their authenticity of what they really want is a difficult one. Unfortunately, sometimes your legitimate job offers can get caught in this process.

Next, sometimes young or inexperienced candidates can be misguided as to how to conduct a salary negotiation. They might be encouraged by friends and relations to be tough and to stick with the really high demand on the mistaken assumption that, "if the organization really wants you, they will pay". However, very few organizations will meet unreasonable salary demands unless there is something truly remarkable about the candidate. If you think that this inexperienced candidate is getting bad advice, you can work with the person and explain the facts of life if you think it worthwhile to you. Of course, by now, you might be questioning whether or not you want a candidate who is influenced unreasonably and may have a stubborn streak. However, remember that salary negotiation is a learned skill. A lot of people just do not know how to do it.

Lastly, you could get a candidate who just wants to get all that can be had out of you. A little bargaining is expected—the question for you is at what point is the bargaining and the demand out of line? Again, is this the personality that you want?

As a footnote to dealing with people who are making and staying with unreasonable salary demands, don't blame yourself that you did not see this in the interview. People behave differently around money and salary and that cannot always be discovered in advance. Be grateful at least that it is showing up now.

Before entering into salary negotiations, make sure that you know the limits of your negotiating power. This is, particularly, a problem in the public sector where there is little room for negotiation. Most jobs in the public sector have a fixed salary range and your negotiating power is very limited.

What if your company does permit more negotiation but you are not the final decision maker on salary? If you are not the final decision-maker, then consult with the person who is, in advance, in order to get that person's approval. Remember that whatever is offered to a candidate in salary is binding so be careful not to overstep your authority.

Within reason, it is better to meet a good percentage of the candidate's demands for a salary. When people come to a job for a lower salary than they think they deserve, there is usually resentment. This is not a good beginning to a person's organizational life. It is not worth the few hundred or, in some cases, the few thousand dollars difference to have a dissatisfied candidate. Of course, you might feel that a candidate does not have to accept the job if he or she has a problem with the salary. Certainly, this is true but people come to jobs for many reasons of which salary may be only a part. The candidate can have pleasure in some parts of the job and disappointment in others. As much as possible, do not make the salary an issue for the candidate's disappointment.

From time to time, we encounter candidates who will tell us that they have another job offer and that the other job is offering a higher salary. If the candidate truly has an offer, again you must weigh whether or not you want the candidate enough to exceed the other offer. Also, try to ascertain which job the candidate is really interested in. Have a frank conversation with the candidate if you can. You want a candidate who is motivated for the job not the higher salary offer. We will discuss this issue in more detail in Point 5.

Now sometimes the candidate will say that there is another offer in an attempt to leverage us to offer a higher salary. If you suspect this—the vagueness of what the candidate is saying sometimes gives him or her away—just hold to the salary offer or withdraw the offer. This is a bad beginning and everyone should be reluctant to hire anyone who plays games like this. Unfortunately, it is rather difficult to detect if the candidate is lying. Sometimes it helps to ask the candidate questions about the other job to see if the candidate is dodging the questions. More often than not, figuring out if the candidate is lying becomes a matter for your intuition.

Be sure not to take advantage of people when negotiating salary. People who are relatively young or inexperienced in salary negotiations can be taken advantage of quite easily, particularly, if they really desire the job. However, it is not long before candidates realize that they were taken advantage of and they will begin to resent you for taking advantage of them. The little bit of financial savings is not worth later employee alienation. Another note of caution here. Sometimes, we say to ourselves "well, the employee agreed to work for that salary and knew what he was getting so why is he complaining now?". The truth is that employees do complain and will complain and will resent you. The fact that they agreed to that salary at that point in time will carry little weight. Very few people have the self-discipline to accept the consequences of their actions. Young and bright employees, in particular, grow quickly on the job and will soon come to understand your actions and think the less of you for it.

There are jobs that do not permit any salary negotiations and the candidate needs to know that early in the interview process. It is very awkward for a candidate to go through the interview thinking that the salary and the benefits are negotiable only to discover at the critical point of offer that they are not. This is particularly important if the advertised salary was below the candidate's expectations but the candidate was led somehow to believe that a higher salary could be negotiated. Unless the job has something very special about it, it is the rare candidate who will take a job at a lower salary.

The candidate is not the only one who has a problem thinking that the salary was negotiable when it was not. You also have a problem on your hands. It is difficult for anyone to come this far in choosing a candidate only to have the candidate withdraw at the last minute because of a misunderstanding. The interview process is a great deal of work and no one wants to spend that kind of time for no result. Make sure that all the candidates know in advance whether or not the salary is negotiable.

Finally, be sure that you have no prejudices when you are negotiating salary. Equal pay must be given for equal work. Women and minorities do not need less money than anyone else.

POINT 3: APPROACH THE CANDIDATE PROPERLY.

The initial contact that you have with the candidate sets the tone for the rest of the negotiations with the candidate. Therefore, make the initial approach to the candidate with skill and warmth. The goodwill that is established will be a firm foundation for a future relationship.

Begin this way. Call the candidate on the phone but, before proceeding with the offer, make sure that the candidate is in a situation in which he or she can talk. The candidate might be in an open office or might have the boss nearby. If the candidate cannot talk at this time, arrange to call at a more convenient time or even at home that evening. It is important that the candidate be in a place where an open conversation can occur. Otherwise, it will be difficult to have a serious discussion with a candidate who does not feel comfortable responding.

Begin by praising the candidate's interview and references. This gives the candidate time to prepare mentally. Then, move rapidly into the job offer. After the initial offer, you should fall silent and let the candidate speak. You will hear surprise, pleasure and sometimes hesitation in the candidate's voice. Listen for these cues as the candidate's initial reaction will tell you what the candidate is really thinking about this job.

Have a lot of patience during this initial conversation with the candidate. The candidate is making a big decision and needs to be completely comfortable before making a change of this magnitude. Answer all of the candidate's questions in a satisfactory manner. Spend all the time that the candidate needs. After all, no one wants to hire a candidate who still has questions or doubts about the job.

Some organizations make a job offer first by letter. This is not without its merits because it lets the candidate know that the offer is firm. However, the initial contact by a letter is a little cool even if subsequent conversations are warm and welcoming. A telephone call is better.

POINT 4: COMPETE EFFECTIVELY WITH OTHER OFFERS.

Occasionally, a good candidate will have more than one offer. This happens often when new graduates are coming out of school—particularly out of professional schools. It also happens when a person has really decided to leave the current job and is making an aggressive job search. Most of the time, when you offer the job, the candidate will tell you about the offer or offers. Ask the candidate what the other job offer is and spend a little time discussing it. Try to get an idea about what the candidate likes about the other position and why there is hesitation about your position. Do be careful not to overstep any boundaries, of course, in asking these questions. After all, you are a future employer not a career counselor. You need basic information so that you can compete effectively with the other offer. After getting a sense of the other job, try to pitch your job without overselling it. It is not wise for the candidate to have a false impression of the organization. However, do discuss what the job has to offer and what the short-term and long-term advantages are of working with you. Be sure to discuss promotional opportunities, management styles, and training and development.

If the candidate is very hesitant and appears to be leaning in the opposite direction, let the candidate go. If a candidate is persuaded against his or her inner judgment, sooner or later the individual will regret the decision and leave the organization anyway.

Sometimes it comes to pass that you feel that the candidate should take the other job. This feeling may take you by surprise. If it occurs that, given the candidate's direction in life, the other job would be better, cease to press the case. After all, if your instincts are correct, the candidate will not be with you for long anyway. Do not withdraw the offer but back off. The final decision is with the candidate.

POINT 5: ACCEPT NO FOR AN ANSWER.

Sometimes in spite of all our best efforts, the candidate refuses the job offer. The candidate may have been completely sincere but after careful thought has decided that this is just not the right job.

In this case, just accept the candidate's decision with goodwill and courtesy. Then move on to your second choice, or if there is no good second choice, start looking again.

POINT 6: NEGOTIATE THE START DATE.

Usually, we want the candidate to come as soon as possible. The candidate also wants to come as soon as possible but needs time to resign properly from the current job. Allow the candidate to give at least two weeks to one month's notice to the current employer. Of course, higher level or academic positions will need much more time than two weeks. Do not hurt your own organization by being too generous with the start date but do allow the candidate to leave the job properly. Everyone needs to leave their current position with good feelings. This is particularly important for a candidate who may have been employed by an organization for a long time.

Do be sensitive to the candidate who has to move into the area. Moving requires a great deal of work, effort and time. Allow the candidate adequate time to look around, find a place and move in. This does not mean that weeks and weeks must be given to the candidate to buy a new house, sell the old one and completely settle down. It simply means that the candidate needs time to find a place to live even if temporarily. It is much easier for candidates, starting a new job, to feel relaxed in their new surroundings as opposed to feeling frantic over being unsettled in their home life. This is particularly true of candidates with kids who must be in new schools or in day care.

Even if a candidate does not have any special needs, you may want to consider giving the candidate some time to just relax between jobs. After all, it will be a year before the candidate gets another vacation and it is in your best interest for the candidate to come to work rested and prepared.

Exhibit as much courtesy as possible on the start date while meeting the needs of your organization. After all, you are developing a long-term relationship with this employee. It pays off in the long run to have a good beginning.

One last thought. Sometimes for unusual circumstances an candidate needs an exceptionally long start date—much longer than would be reasonable for the position. In this situation, weigh how much you want the candidate against the needs of the organization. Be aware, though, that if you wait too long, there is a great chance that the candidate will never take the job. The longer the candidate delays the more chance that even more variables will emerge that will affect the candidate's employment with your organization.

POINT 7: GIVE TIME FOR CONSIDERATION.

No candidate should accept a job on the spur of the moment. Even if the candidate does say yes right away, give the candidate an evening to think it over. Many times a decision looks a little different in the morning.

Most candidates will ask you for a few days to think it over. Give the candidate a week at the most to consider the offer. If you can, include a weekend in that time so that the candidate can really give the job move some relaxed thought. A week is long enough time to consider. If the candidate is taking longer than a week then there is a likelihood that the candidate is having problems with the job offer. There is also the likelihood that the candidate is waiting for another job offer to come through and is stalling for time. The candidate may want the other job more but may not want to lose your opportunity if the other job does not come through. If the candidate is taking too long, inquire as to what further information is needed to help to make a decision. However, it is easier if a deadline for acceptance or refusal is agreed upon at the same time that the job offer is made. After that, unless the candidate gives a good reason for delay, the job offer should be withdrawn. Never wait on a candidate who has too much ambivalence about the job.

Do consider the organization's needs in giving the candidate time for consideration. After all, if you wait too long, you might lose other good candidates who wanted the position.

POINT 8: MAKE SPECIAL ARRANGEMENTS.

Since life does not come to a stop whenever a job offer occurs, sometimes people need special arrangements for previously scheduled events. The most frequent of these is vacation for which the tickets and hotel are bought and paid for. Usually, in this case, the candidate agrees to a start date but needs to go on vacation shortly after arrival. Be flexible on this. A couple of weeks will not make much difference in the long run.

There are two other areas in which people may need special arrangements after starting work. Some candidates might be taking a degree, learning a language, or be enrolled in some other form of educational opportunity. They may need to leave work early for awhile, take a longer lunch or arrive later. As long as this is not a permanent situation, be flexible. After all, an educated person is of benefit to every organization.

The special arrangment that does involve flexibility for the long-term is child care. When the kids have to be picked up or dropped off at certain times, it places a limit on the candidate's working hours. Kids are a fact of life so try to work this out with the candidate in a way that is mutually satisfactory. Do be careful to ascertain the ramifications of agreeing to some special arrangements. Sometimes managers feel generous towards a new employee and agree to more than can be really handled. Think about the implications of what is being asked, the precedent that is being set in the organization, and whether or not the organization can deliver over the long-term.

POINT 9: DEMONSTRATE COURTESY.

Do demonstrate as much courtesy as possible to the candidate who is moving into the area. If you can, assist a candidate who will be relocating for the job if the person is not familiar with the area.

The new employee should be advised where to stay while looking for a place to live. The new person should also receive information about the city which can include newspapers, maps, schools, and referrals to real estate agents. Give the new person a tour of the city and show the areas that might be a good place to live. In short, really help out. This will greatly help a new employee transition into the job.

POINT 10: CONFIRM IN WRITING.

Do follow-up the job offer in writing. This letter should specifiy all of the terms of employment including start date, salary, benefits, special arrangements, status, and time limitations on the position. The letter guarantees that there is no misunderstanding regarding employment. The letter also gives the candidate the security of a firm offer. In fact, there are some candidates who will not accept a position until it is in writing.

CONCLUSION

The candidate needs to have a positive experience when receiving a job offer. This holds true even if the candidate is extremely interested in the position and will accept the job no matter what. Wrangles over start dates, salary, and other matters make the employee's entrance into the organization an unpleasant one. That initial negative feeling can stay with the candidate for a very long time and can be the seeds of later alienation from the organization.

Handle the job offer as professionally as you would all other aspects of the interview. The offer of the job, and its implications to you and the candidate alike, are extremely serious and should not be regarded in a casual fashion. Make every effort to present a good job offer if you want to net good candidates.

OFFERING THE JOB

QUICK CHECK

Point 1: Prepare the offer.

- Did you plan what to say to the candidate?
- Can you answer the candidate's questions?
- Did you treat the offer with respect?
- Have you consulted with your boss?

Point 2: Negotiate salary effectively.

- Has the salary been determined in advance?
- Do you have the authority to offer a higher salary?
- Do you want to match the candidate's demands?
- Is the candidate being honest about other job offers?
- Is the candidate making unreasonable salary demands?

Point 3: Approach the candidate properly.

- Was the candidate called at an appropriate time?
- Did the candidate have time to ask questions?
- Should the offer be made by letter?

Point 4: Compete effectively with other offers.

- Does the candidate have more than one offer?
- Is the other offer better for the candidate?
- Did you present your offer in a favorable but realistic light?

Point 5: Accept no for an answer.

- Did you accept the candidate's decision with goodwill and courtesy?

Point 6: Negotiate the start date.

- Does the candidate have time to leave the old job properly?
- Does the candidate need time to move?
- Does the candidate need vacation time?
- Does the candidate need any other special arrangements?

Point 7: Give time for consideration.

- Does the candidate have enough time to think over the job?
- Is the candidate taking too long to think it over?

Point 8: Make special arrangements.

- Does the candidate have a vacation planned?
- Is the candidate taking classes?
- Does the candidate have child care issues?

Point 9: Demonstrate courtesy.

- Does the candidate need help moving?
- Does the candidate have enough information about the city?
- Did you send information about the city to the candidate?

Point 10: Confirm in writing.

- Has the candidate been sent a letter to confirm the appointment?
- Does the letter spell out all of the terms of employment?

8 WRAPPING UP THE INTERVIEW PROCESS

POINTS TO REMEMBER

Point 1: Inform all candidates who were not selected.
Point 2: Inform all candidates in a timely fashion.
Point 3: Announce the appointment.
Point 4: Manage hostile responses.
Point 5: Manage special concerns.
Point 6: Evaluate the interview.

WRAPPING UP THE INTERVIEW PROCESS

Once the interview is over and the candidate has accepted, our natural impulse is to bring the interview process to a close. After all, the next project is waiting and there is little time in our busy lives for more details. However, bringing the interview process to an end just because the candidate has accepted is premature. There is still some work left to be done. In fact, the interview process should not be seen as complete until all the points in this chapter are wrapped up. Let's look now at what is left to be done to complete the interview process.

POINT 1: INFORM ALL CANDIDATES WHO WERE NOT SELECTED.

Be sure to inform all of the candidates who were not selected of your decision. Since the candidates have taken the trouble to prepare and interview for the job, the least that we can do is to let them know what has happened. To keep them ignorant of the outcome of something of so much importance to them is discourteous and unprofessional.

Why is it that so often candidates are not informed of the dispostion of a job? There are four main reasons for this failure. First, and most often, is just sloppiness on our parts. Following-through completely to the end of a process is a problem that many of us have particularly when more interesting or more pressing projects are on the horizon. Second, we dislike dealing with the distress that disappointed candidates sometimes have. No one wants to handle the upset of disappointed candidates. It is not easy to tell people something that will hurt them. Third, we sometimes are uncomfortable with the anger that rejected candidates can have. We have all had the unpleasant situation of being confronted by the tough questions of candidates wanting to know why they were not chosen. Moreover, these questions, which usually are versions of "why was I not good enough", are sometimes difficult to answer particularly when people are upset. Fourth, we are sometimes careless of other people's feelings. Since we see so much coming and going in the hiring process, we forget that not everyone has developed our sophisticated viewpoint. Inexperienced candidates, in particular, are not as accustomed to the disappointment and occasional harshness of the process.

If you have been failing to inform candidates about the job, put yourself in the shoes of the candidates and consider their feelings. Once you think about the situation from the candidates' point of view, you will not neglect to let the candidates know what has happened with the job.

Make sure that the proper method is chosen for informing the candidates. There are two ways to inform candidates — by writing to them or speaking to them. Let's look at writing to the candidates first.

When we consider writing a letter to the candidates we must keep in mind whether the candidates are from outside your organization or from the inside, that is to say, already working for your company.

Candidates, from the outside, who are not known to you before the interview and about whom you did not feel strongly can receive a politely worded letter informing them of your decision. A letter is easier on you emotionally than having to call each candidate. Keep the letter brief and to the point, express no regrets and no explanation of the decision. A possible phrasing is:

"Thank you for your interest in a position with X company. Although we have selected another candidate for the X position, we enjoyed our interview with you. We wish you every success in the future."

Such a letter will usually elicit one of four responses. More often than not, you will never hear from the candidate again. Most candidates will simply move on with their job search elsewhere. Sometimes you will get a nicely worded letter back thanking you for the opportunity to interview and asking to be considered in the future. Once in awhile you will get a not so nicely worded letter that protests or criticizes your decision. Be grateful that you did not select that candidate. Sometimes you will get a phone call from the candidate who will want to know why you made the decision that you made. We will talk more about that in just a moment.

Now what about writing a letter to candidates who are inside your organization? In general, I recommend against it since colleagues do deserve the special courtesy of hearing from you in person. The personal touch is very important for future relationships—after all, even if the candidate did not get the job, you still want him or her to think well about you and about the process.

Let's look now at what happens when you decide to speak with candidates either face-to-face or over the phone.

Whether the candidates are inside or outside candidates, there is the same sequence of events. First and most important, start by thinking through what you are going to say before you make that call or see that person. A conversation rejecting a candidate can be quite difficult sometimes so it is important that you be prepared mentally for whatever might occur. Lower your voice to relay to the candidate that bad news is coming. Then, thank the candidate for interviewing. Without wasting more time, move rapidly to telling the candidate that another was selected. Praise what can be praised or, at least, speak positively, and thank the candidate for his or her interest in the position. The candidate can be encouraged to reapply for other positions if you intend to really consider the person but, of course, the encouragement must be done without any promises.

While speaking with the candidate, at no time express any regret for the decision. The candidate needs to know that there is no room for negotiating the decision. Some disappointed candidates may try to get a change of mind from you. Other candidates may be angry about the decision and may complain and protest. Just weather this conversation and continue to be fair but firm. Fortunately, most rejected candidates handle the bad news very graciously.

Be completely prepared for candidates to ask you immediately why they did not get the job. You should decide in advance if you want to discuss this in detail or not. With outside candidates that were not known to you before the interview it is better to simply respond in a superficial but not frivolous manner. Rarely can outside candidates, who have no relationship with you, handle an in-depth conversation. Additionally, you do not know the candidate well so you will not have any idea of how the candidate is handling the information. Inside candidates are a different matter. For them, you should be prepared to say briefly why they were not selected because this is important for their personal development.

If the inside candidate is someone who really shows promise, consider offering to speak with the candidate at a future date about the interview so that the individual can learn how to develop more in terms of job preparation and interview skills. You should only make this offer to someone that you know well enough, you think is mature enough, or is motivated enough to handle a conversation of this kind. Naturally, this future conversation should be at the initiative of the candidate but many candidates looking to get ahead will take you up on your offer.

Do make a distinction between speaking face-to-face or calling a person on the phone. Obviously, outside candidates or inside candidates at another location than yourself, should receive a phone call. For inside candidates at your work location, it is nicer to see them in person. The exception to this is when you know that the person will take the information hard and may have an initial emotional reaction. It may be easier on the person if you do not see his or her first expression of upset. In this case, use the telephone to help the person to save face.

Either in person or on the phone, the candidates will appreciate your extra effort and courtesy and appreciate that you took the time to inform them yourself.

As a rule of thumb, remember that the method that you choose, whether writing or speaking, is a measure of the closeness and interest that you have in the candidate. The closer and more interested you are, the more likely the personal touch.

POINT 2: INFORM ALL CANDIDATES IN A TIMELY FASHION.

It is important also to convey your decision about the job in a timely fashion to the candidates who were not selected. Let's look at this from the point of view of the candidate who was from outside of your organization and of the candidate who was already working for your organization.

It is not fair to keep outside candidates waiting and waiting to hear about the job once you have made your decision. If candidates can make the effort to submit a resume, prepare for and have an interview, all in a timely manner, then you can certainly make the effort to let them know what has happened as soon as it happened. This lets the candidates move on and continue their search elsewhere.

Inside candidates are a different matter. The greatest problem with inside candidates is reaching them before they hear about the appointment elsewhere. No candidates should hear about the job from anyone but you. Often when you are not the first to reach the candidates, the candidates hear about the decision in a setting that is awkward for them. For example, if they are in a meeting and hear publically that someone else was appointed, it could be a very embarrassing for them. No one wants their internal candidates embarrassed by hearing from the wrong source. It is hurtful to the candidates and damages any future relationship that you might have with the candidates.

Now, information about who was selected for a job travels like wildfire in an organization. So how do we reach the disappointed candidates first and stop the information about the appointment from traveling ahead of us? First, make sure that only key people know who was selected. Second, ask the candidate who was selected not to make public comments until you have time to inform all candidates. Of course, you do need to reach all of the candidates within a couple of hours because it is not fair to ask the newly chosen person to sit on information like that. Do not be disappointed if word gets out anyway. Information of this kind is just too good to keep quiet for most people. However, keep emphasizing to staff over and over, interview after interview, the importance of keeping such information private until all candidates can be reached. Sooner or later, an organization that can keep such a secret will emerge and you will have fewer and fewer people who get hurt by hearing about job appointments from the wrong source.

POINT 3: ANNOUNCE THE APPOINTMENT.

After all the candidates have been informed, proceed to announce the appointment to the rest of the staff. Immediate staff that will be affected by the position should be told first. After that, it is nice to send out a short memo to the rest of the organization telling about the appointment, the person's qualifications and history and the start date.

If the person is high enough or in a public position, press releases can also be sent to professional journals or to the newspapers.

POINT 4: MANAGE HOSTILE RESPONSES.

Every once in awhile, there will be a response from an unsuccessful candidate that is completely inappropriate. This inappropriateness can take many forms such as harassing phone calls and hostile letters to you or to the successful candidate. Nasty letters may be sent to elected officials or to the press or to the President of your company. Even inappropriate visits to you may occur.. I even had relatives of the candidate visit me once! The list of ways for people to behave inappropriately is endless and is as varied and as imaginative as the human race.

If this occurs, consider first of all whether or not the candidate is an outside or an inside candidate. If the person is outside, and the aggravation is annoying but non-threatening, you may just want to let it die down and go away. Most of the time, this person's anger will dissapate or will move onto something else. If the situation continues or feels threatening to you in anyway, both the police and your company's attorney's should get involved. Your job is to protect yourself and the people in your organization if you have had the misfortune to encounter such an unbalanced candidate.

The inside candidate who goes off the deep end is quite a different matter. In this instance, speak with that person's supervisor immediately, with your boss, and with the personnel office if you have one. This employee needs counseling. The form of disciplinary action, depending upon the severity of the response, should include the the possibility of dismissal. Unfortunately, these actions could also aggravate the situation but of course, no organization can tolerate this type of behavior from an employee.

POINT 5: MANAGE SPECIAL CONCERNS.

There are a number of special problems that can emerge whenever candidates are not selected for the job. Anticipate these problems and their responses because these problems can occur at any time.

The first of these is the dilemma that is created when the favorite candidate was not hired.

Why is a favorite candidate sometimes not selected? There are two main reasons. First, a favorite candidate is usually a favorite for a good reason, meaning that the candidate has demonstrated a lot of promise in the past. You might just think that the promise was not developed enough for the job. Second, the favorite candidate can sometimes get knocked out by a stellar interview performance from someone from the outside or a dark horse candidate from the inside. Both are legitimate reasons to not select the favorite.

What is the reaction of the favorite candidate and how do you handle it? Usually, the individual is surprised, puzzled, embarrassed, and disappointed. Don't be conciliatory but do spend some time—although not immediately because emotions need time to die down—with this candidate so that he or she can understand what were the weaknesses in performance, promise, or interview that caused him or her not to be selected. Mostly, you do not want to alienate this individual who clearly has ability. Therefore, work with this candidate so that the next time has a successful outcome.

Now, it is possible that your overtures might be rejected if the candidate is very angry. If the candidate cannot get past this emotion, you should just let the person go and note it for the future—

this is a character weakness. Personally, I would be very reluctant to promote this person in the future.

Then there is the reaction of staff when the favorite candidate was not selected. Remember that a vacant position is like a thoroughbred race. Everyone has their money down on the nose of a favorite candidate. When the favorite candidate is not appointed, everyone is taken by surprise. That surprise leads to several days of gossip and speculation. In this case, remember that you do not need to explain yourself to every quarter of the organization no matter what your reasons were for not appointing the favorite. Don't be defensive. Just move forward with your decision. The gossip, some of which will be unfavorably directed towards you, will shortly die down anyway. You may want to strategically leak a couple of comments to staff to help this process along—not enough comments to injure the integrity of the interview but enough to indicate that your reasons were sound. It also helps if you speak openly and positively, but not defensively, of the successful candidate while being sensitive to the disappointed candidate. If the gossip is getting to you a bit, remember that there will be many reasonable, if less vocal, people who will have already recognized and acknowledged some of the weaknesses of the favorite candidate that stopped you from appointing that person in the first place. Continue to deal with the favorite nicely through this period but never in an apologetic fashion. Business as usual should be the watchword whenever you confront this situation.

The second problem is when you have to deal with any inside candidates who decide to get angry because they were not selected. These candidates, and sometimes their buddies, might give you the cold shoulder, make sarcastic remarks, or exhibit other forms of immature behavior. Some of it, assuming it is not blatant, you can just pretend not to notice. Ignore it and go about your business and be sure to congratulate yourself on not selecting them for the job. Most of this childish behavior from candidates and friends will go away in a couple of days when people remember that they might want to have future promotions or keep the job they do have. If the childish behavior continues and immediately threatens to embarrass you or your reputation in anyway, or if it crosses the line into hostile actions, then you have an employee discipline problem on your hands. Act on it. Employees cannot continue to affect and infect the workplace negatively.

The third problem is when the person who was acting in the job was not selected for the permanent position. Be concerned with that person's feelings and the need of that individual to save face.

It is very embarrassing to have been acting in a job, to apply for the position permanently and to be turned down. This candidate would naturally assume that there was a problem or some failure in the way that he or she did the job. You should let the acting person know why he or she was not selected. Through understanding, most people can be reconciled to decisions and can also begin to understand the skills needed to succeed in the future.

However, be prepared for a 98% probability that the acting person will be angry at you even if he or she is behaving professionally and not showing anger. The anger of disappointed acting candidates is a special kind of anger. The loss of a job that a person actually held is a very personal thing and the loss of it will almost certainly be taken personally. Just remember that the anger is there, even if you cannot see it, and sooner or later it will manifest itself. Often, it will show up later in some form of disloyalty to you. It is a rare person who can have the objectivity and personal insight to understand why he or she did not get the job.

Staff will also have a reaction when the acting candidate does not get the job. They may feel that you really have been unfair for not selecting the acting person. Just act normally and give people time to come around. Neither intrude nor exclude yourself from being around the acting candidate nor the disgruntled staff. If the hiring decision was really sound, the reasonable people eventually will have understanding of it. Of course, once again, you should not tolerate any of this disgruntlement for too long and never if it disrespects your person or your reputation.

POINT 6: EVALUATE THE INTERVIEW.

Managing the interview successfully is one of the most critical skills that you can possess. A successful interview process means that good people are hired. When good people are hired, the organization has tremendous potential for success.

Don't think of managing the interview as an isolated incident. Learn from each interview that you have in order to continually improve your skills and the skills of the organization.

Evaluate, evaluate, evaluate how you did in managing the interview. Did the questions elicit enough information about the candidate? Were the logistics of the interview handled well? Were the candidates properly screened? Did the announcement of the chosen candidate go well? In other words, play back the interview process in your mind and be very realistic in your evaluation. Think about the things that you did well and the things that you would like to improve on next time.

You may want to consider writing notes to yourself about things in the interview process that you would like to improve on. Keep this in a file that you actually find again. This can be reviewed the next time you have to manage an interview.

Lastly, remember the one true measure of the successful interview—was the candidate who was selected successful on the job?

CONCLUSION

Congratulations! You have just successfully concluded the interview process.

WRAPPING UP

QUICK CHECK

Point 1: Inform all candidates who were not selected.

- Were all the candidates informed of the decision?
- Are you afraid of confronting disappointed candidates?
- Will you be sending a letter or speaking to the candidate?
- Are you mentally prepared to talk to the candidate?
- Are you going to talk to the candidate about the interview?

Point 2: Inform all candidates in a timely fashion.

- Have you let all the candidates know about the job in a timely fashion?
- Did the inside candidates hear about the job from anyone but you?

Point 3: Announce the appointment.

- Was everyone most affected by the position informed first?
- Was a memo sent out?
- Are press releases necessary?

Point 4: Manage hostile responses.

- Is the candidate unable to accept the decision?
- Are you feeling harassed by a candidate?
- Is legal action needed?

Point 5: Manage special concerns.

- Is the favorite candidate upset over not getting the job?
- Are internal candidates angry about not getting the job?
- Is the acting candidate upset over not getting the job?
- Are you allowing the gossip to die down?
- Are you behaving in a normal fashion even though staff is angry?
- Have the angry candidates been given distance until they cool off?
- Do you need to take any disciplinary action over angry staff?

Point 6: Evaluate the interview.

- Do you know how could the interview be improved?
- Did you make a note of the things that you would like to improve?
- Have mistakes been faced realistically?
- Is the candidate that was selected successful on the job?

AFTERWORD

The demands of doing business today are very great. No matter in what type of organization we find ourselves, we now face a more diversified, more accelerated and more changeable environment than ever before. We have only to look back as little as forty years ago to see the changes. At that time, the issues of rapid technological growth, population shifts, global economies, massive information production and declining resources were little considered. Now, every organization faces rapid changes in its technology, in its services and in its products in a world of global competition, unstable finances and instantaneous communication.

It is our dilemma to be faced with such changes and yet have to continue to deliver the highest level of service or product possible. How can we be successful in such an environment?

As we have seen in this book, one way that we ensure success is to hire the best staff possible. The survival of an organization rests upon the ability of the staff to guide an organization successfully through challenging environments. It is in our best interests to obtain the most qualified, and the most dedicated, staff possible. However, we cannot hire the best staff unless we manage the interview well. When we learn how to manage the interview well, we dramatically increase our ability to hire the best staff.

Remember to follow the points that we have outlined in this book when you are interviewing. Each of these points will help you to manage the interview successfully.

The interview is a challenging process. Give the interview process both attention and commitment.

What will be your reward for so much work? Your reward will be when you see your chosen candidate successful on the job and making a real contribution to your organization.

INDEX

Dr. Susan C. Curzon is the Vice-Provost of Information and Technology Resources and Dean of the University Library at California State University, Northridge. She has held a variety of management positions including the Director of Libraries for the Glendale Public Library in Glendale, California and as a Regional Administrator for the County of Los Angeles Public Library. Her doctorate is in Public Administration from the University of Southern California. Her M.L.S. is from the University of Washington. She is the author of a previous book entitled "Managing Change: A How-To-Do-It Manual for Planning, Implementing and Evaluating Change in Libraries".